38763

D1250419

MY FATHER

MY FATHER

An Intimate Portrait of

DWIGHT MOODY

By

PAUL D. MOODY

Illustrated

BOSTON

LITTLE, BROWN AND COMPANY

1938

THE ATLANTIC MONTHLY PRESS BOOKS
ARE PUBLISHED BY
LITTLE, BROWN AND COMPANY
IN ASSOCIATION WITH
THE ATLANTIC MONTHLY COMPANY

To my sister

PREFACE

"No public man is less understood, especially by the thinking world, than D. L. Moody," wrote Henry Drummond in 1894. Now, after more than half a lifetime, it is still true. No complete picture of him has been drawn and this is certainly no attempt. It is rather a series of informal snapshots taken through the lens of a boy's eye. It is no attempt at an objective study or an appraisal of the man or the work he did. From the day when as a small boy I shared the usual feeling of small boys that "my father is a hundred times stronger and richer than yours," to the present day, he has seemed the greatest man and the best man I have ever known. "Perfect love casteth out fear," and I, knowing what he really was, have never been afraid to see how he looked to other men. I am aware of the criticisms which have been made of him both by his friends and by those who did not agree with him. I have read, if not all, most of the things that have been written about him. There are some fifty-six or more biographies and none of them have completely captured him. I certainly cannot do it. This is only an attempt to record some of the things I saw him do and heard him say for the sake alike of the few remaining who knew and loved him and of the many who never knew or saw him. Except for the sake of continuity or elucidation I have tried to leave unrepeated what has been written by others. If his figure moves a little more out of the mist, I shall be satisfied.

We can only write of another as he seems to us, and can never know the ultimate truth. Every biography is but partial. God alone knows all. Even the sum of our various knowledges is not the full truth.

It will be said this is a very partial and one-sided record. Of course it is. I am only telling what he seemed like to me, his son, in the too brief years in which I lived with him.

P. D. M.

September 1937

CONTENTS

ILLUSTRATIONS

MY FATHER

I

THE COUNTRY LIFE

FOR those remarkable people who could remember vividly events which happened when they were two years old or less, I have had a great deal of envy, modified by greater skepticism. In the case of my own lack of vivid early impressions I have comforted myself by saying that veracity was better than memory. Try my best, I can recall nothing before I was at least five save shadowy impressions which never do articulate with fixed events. As a tot I was taken to England on my father's second mission there in 1881–1883, but apart from a vague memory of a Christmas at Pau, where my mother had taken us for my brother's sake (for he was not strong), I remember nothing. But Pau does stand out in my recollections, for Father visited us at Christmas at the pension where we were staying and I remember indistinctly my mother coaching him in one or two French phrases which he wanted to use. The roars of laughter which greeted his attempts to use them in the dining room and the good-natured teasing he underwent when we returned to our apartment still come to my mind. Later I learned that when he had tried to say "*Bon jour*" to an elderly lady, everybody declared it sounded like "*Mon cher*." And I presume it did, for, having inherited from him a certain deafness to shades of sound, I can easily understand the mistake. And I also remember being taken in the arms of a certain retired army officer as we were sailing home. He proceeded to lie down on the deck and roll over and over with me cradled in his arms. This I thought highly exciting. Poor stuff to salvage from the dim recesses of memory! It is the best I can do. But if my memory was not particularly impressionable, what passes for my mind seems to have been active. Two stories used to be told at my expense.

One my father often recalled with great delight. He and I were driving about the streets of Northfield when I was at a very tender age,

and he was amusing himself by asking me who lived in the various houses, and when I informed him, according to my limited knowledge, he pressed me for information as to their occupations. When our own familiar house appeared

he asked who lived there and I am afraid I said
not too respectfully, "D. L. Moody," and on
being queried as to his occupation I replied,
"He is a sort of preacher," a reply which
pleased my father very much — a great deal
more than it has pleased me when I have heard
the story retold. He declared it described him
very aptly.

The other, of which, needless to say, I have
no recollection, is that on one occasion I was
taken, with some member of my family, to see
King's College Chapel at Cambridge. I have
been told that after looking all about I asked,
"Where is the quiry room?" — the nearest approach to "inquiry" my childish tongue could
make. I cite this not as a criticism of Anglican-
ism or the architecture or use of King's College Chapel, but as an evidence of the early
background of a small boy whose only con-
ception of worship was identified with evangelistic services. I am sure that at that early
day I would never have been permitted in an
"inquiry" room — a room, I might say for the
benefit of the non-evangelistically reared, given

over to those who, aroused in the regular meetings conducted by my father, were to be dealt with by workers who gave advice and answered questions. But at a very early age I knew of the existence of such things. The story, I admit, has nearly lost its point when told to-day, but it shows the outlook of at least one small child in the early eighties and a certain deplorable priggishness which I hope I have long since outgrown.

It is at Northfield I remember my father first most distinctly and as a nearly ideal companion for a very small boy. The interest he took in the affairs of his son would have flattered the son had he been old enough to appreciate it. The fact that ten years separated me from my brother (and my sister was older than my brother) left me in the position almost of belonging to a second family. And in those years, I see now, far more clearly than I saw then, that my father was, whenever he was at home, making up to me for the lack of any children at home of my age. He had a most engaging way of treating a child, at least he always did me, as if I were more or less his equal in years. He never, to my recollection, talked down to me, but flattered me with the constant assumption that my opinion was sought and that he was interested in what I thought or had to say.

One of my earliest memories is of his extraordinary patience and kindliness and sympathy when I had my first and only impulse as a builder. To the north of our house, abetted by some little playmates seven or eight years old, I gathered some packing boxes and boards and proceeded to build what I conceived to be a barn. My experience of barns being limited to the type then common in New England, it rambled. Box was added to box and joined by very unevenly sawed planks. Even after fifty years I wince at what it must have looked like and marvel at the patience which allowed such a heterogeneous collection of odds and ends to litter up the environs of the home, about which my father was normally rather exacting. Not only was my barn seriously in the way but it must have been a dreadful nuisance. Hammers, saws, and other implements were requisitioned and lost. I was as proud of the monstrosity and as resentful of interference as any artist. Finally even I declared it completed and then my father entered the game. We were going to have a ceremony, he said, like the laying of a cornerstone. I do not remember much of the ceremony except that since a conference was in session there were many people there, which, in view of the labor I had expended, I thought highly proper. But I do remember two things. One was a song written for the occasion by D. B. Towner, which I regret to say was not preserved. After all these years I remember only two lines of the chorus, which at that time seemed to me extremely beautiful and fitting: —

I builded a barn, I builded a barn,
My barn was the largest on Papa's whole farm.

And Henry Drummond, who was there, then proceeded to read telegrams of regret for their absence from the great of the world, including, I remember distinctly, Queen Victoria. I was of an age to be greatly touched by this, though somewhat puzzled. That Queen Victoria should know about my father was not in the least surprising, and of course my barn was a matter of tremendous importance, but nevertheless I was perhaps skeptical for the first time in my life. I was certainly not convinced. Of course the others, including the President, at that time Grover Cleveland, might quite well have known about it, so exalted a position did my father hold in my eyes, and anything his son did would, of course, interest them. But the Queen of England was a shade too much.

Then ice cream and lemonade and cake were served and the party in some way or another manœuvred around to the west of the house, where what should there be but a pair of black goats harnessed into a little wagon which they were dragging up the driveway. Forgotten were the barn, the guests, the amazing telegrams, and even the ice cream.

I suppose this was the beginning of equestrianism, if you can so classify the handling of goats. I learned to harness and unharness the unruly brutes, but I never developed anything save a strictly utilitarian attitude toward them. I have never put a bit in a horse's mouth with a tithe of the difficulty that I experienced in harnessing these animals, and while I have never become exactly companionable with a cow or pig, however much I may have in common with the latter, it is my deep-seated conviction that for purposes of companionship the goat probably rates lower than any other animal. This pair, while no hope of glory, were certainly a means of grace, and to this day I recall too vividly an experience when one of the beasts matched my effort to get a bit into his mouth with an equal determination to get his long and, to me, utterly useless horn into my ear.

But I am not primarily as concerned with the goats as I am with my father's keen delight in the pleasure they afforded me and his enjoyment of the surprise. It was so utterly typical of him, and none of my partners in the enterprise of the barn, nor I myself, derived half the pleasure from the day that my father did. Looking back upon it, I am persuaded that it was a clever attempt to divert my interest from the barn. It worked. The barn was soon condemned, but for a long time I fought its removal. Like much indigenous and primitive architecture, it had to give way to progress.

I do not remember for how long I drove those goats. I do remember that they were turned over to another youngster, who, I think, was crippled. If the goats treated him as they had treated me, his latter estate was worse than his first. But I was promoted to a pony. The winter and spring before I was ten were spent by Father in preaching missions in the West, and on our return I found awaiting us at the station a black pony with four white feet and a white nose and a dog cart. The pony was really a little horse, and while small in stature he was great of heart and I learned to fall off his back with alacrity and enthusiasm. All summer long he was my inseparable companion. His name was Toppy and only once did he show any lack of understanding. That was when, wearing, *à la* cowboy, a wide sombrero, I attempted, for reasons now unremembered, to crawl under him on all fours. The wide rim of my hat tickled his belly and he showed pardonable, but controlled, disapproval.

It was part of my father's plan to accustom us to horses. My sister had hers and my brother his, and I my pony. Many people have commented on my father's love for horses and his marked preference for those with speed. Before I was born, General Julius J. Estey, one of his closest friends, either purchased for him or presented him with a gray mare, "Nellie Gray," which many remember. She lived to a good old age and served my father well and presented him with three colts; one, like herself, a mare of speed and dependability, the two others the most awkward and unmanageable pieces of horseflesh I ever knew. On one occasion I recall, including the colts, there were fourteen horses tied in the old barn, all driving horses, for we did no regular farming. Father was, despite his fondness for horses, no acute judge of them and could easily be imposed upon. He once purchased three at the same time. We watched them brought in the driveway, two men hanging at each horse's head, and the horses on their hind legs. We were warned about driving them. But we did not need the warning, for it soon developed that they had all been doped in some way and were far from being either spirited or energetic. Until Father died he always kept two pairs, one usually steady and the other with more life and action. He preferred to drive the latter pair and he preferred to do the driving. No sitting in a carriage for him while someone else held the reins! He had only one rule about horses. They, like everyone else, should have one day of rest. It did not need to be Sunday, but there must be one day of absolute rest. He used a horse as he used himself, driving with speed. He once remarked that he was too considerate of a horse; my brother was worse yet, and I was the most unreasonable of the family, for I was continually in protest against what I thought was overdriving. He was probably right, for none of the horses ever suffered.

A drive with him, particularly in a buggy, was an experience. The buggy seat was narrow. He was stout and he used to declare that I took up "more than half my share." He disregarded roads and drove across lots or over fields in the most carefree way, and he would drive without a qualm on side hills on which you expected momentarily to see him spilt. And you would be laughed at as foolishly timid if you protested. His favorite hour for driving was early in the morning in the summer, and when the rest of us arrived at breakfast we knew he had been up, sometimes working in his study, but more often just driving about for two or three hours.

One horse in that barn certainly never really belonged there. A wealthy friend wrote and asked Father if he would accept a horse as a present. It was explained that the horse had such action that the hard paved streets of the city injured his hoofs and he needed the country roads. He was accepted and arrived accompanied by an English groom. His name was Roderick and that describes him. He was a large gray with handsome head and neck and the most exaggerated Hackney knee action I have ever seen. He would have been conspicuous in any show ring. And he always moved with dignity, not to say pomp. Somewhere in his ancestry there must have been an English butler. But nothing we could do could persuade him to move faster than a slow, solemn pace. He was positively incongruous on the country roads in the very simple rigs with which our carriage house was stocked. Father attempted to drive him two or three times. His perpendicular motion was faster than his horizontal, and he drove Father to despair and was soon relegated to the other members of the family, who would use him only when every other horse was out. He would make normally almost three miles an hour. Urged, he might do three and a half, and he drove my impetuous father nearly frantic, for Father drove a horse to get somewhere, not merely to watch its stylish knee action.

But his fondness for animals was by no means confined to horses. John Wanamaker

A Drive with Him Was an Experience

once gave him a pair of English mastiffs. When things were busiest, the female would have a litter of pups, and they were large litters. Then would begin the work of distributing them. Years afterwards evidence of mastiff blood could be seen in mongrels on back farms around Northfield. When I was a small boy he had had deer in a high, enclosed paddock behind the house. These disappeared when a buck attacked me and threw me down. Once he had pheasants, and a special house was built for them; and I have dim recollections of peacocks. My memory of the swans is unfortunately not so dim. He thought they would lend an air to a near-by pond and he ordered a pair. Not only were they forever escaping to the river and necessitating a concentrated drive by everyone he could commandeer to recapture them, but in the winter he built a long hut for them over a brook, a mile from the house. In order that they might swim in water free from ice, for one long winter my brother and I stoked a fire in that hut. It really was n't practical. At all our remonstrances he would chuckle, thinking that we were getting too soft.

Swans and peacocks and pheasants were nothing, however, to hens. Now a hen always seemed to me one of the least responsive of all created things. But Father loved them, not individually but in the mass, and he had hundreds of them, usually at least a mile from the house, fortunately, which necessitated two or more men giving their entire time to them. It may have been that after a winter of crowded meetings their very unresponsiveness made an appeal to him. He loved to get into an old pair of rubber boots and an utterly disreputable hat and trousers and waistcoat, much too light colored, and a brown velveteen jacket, and go and feed more corn to his overfed hens. His family called this outfit the "bumblebee suit" and it was a welcome escape from the more formal and almost black suits he wore the rest of the time. The man who is careless of his attire all the time never knows the value of contrast. It is the fastidious man who tastes to

18

the full the pleasure of letting go. And this my father did.

Here is the explanation of the difference between formal pictures of my father and snapshots. When preaching, he was meticulous about having his hair and beard well trimmed. He neglected them shockingly and boyishly when *en repos*, and this was when snapshots were taken at Northfield. But in all other matters he was as fastidious as any man I have ever known and took as many baths daily as a Roman noble in the decadent period. Only he took them as cold as he could get them two or three times a day, or oftener. I lived in constant fear that he would want ice in them and I should have to bring it up. But the doctors finally put a stop to the intensely cold baths, as being a shock to his heart, and he reluctantly resigned himself to water too cold for most people but not cold enough for polar bears or himself.

He liked to lure members of the family into riding with him to the hen yard. We displayed a regrettable reluctance. After one or two trips we discovered that our function was to hold the horse while he held endless, wordless communication with his wretched hens. We used to stipulate when he asked us to go driving that we would go if he was not going to call on his beloved poultry. Sometimes he would sigh and take us in. At other times he would grin shame-facedly and drive off for another victim.

Occasionally he would sell some hens or some eggs. On these occasions he would glee-fully boast as to how much he had made. Then the secret was to look at my mother, who paid all the bills, and her face was a study. She had early abandoned the attempt to argue with him or point out that she was paying out money for labor and grain which must have brought the price of those eggs up to siege value. In short, the most practical of men, he reveled in being as utterly impractical as he wanted to be at play. It was an escape, a release, and he made the most of it.

The donkeys should not be forgotten. Father conceived the idea when he returned from

Palestine, where donkeys were common, that they would be picturesque in Northfield, which they certainly were. He bought one which soon foaled and we had two. He thought they might be useful dragging the lawn mower, but it was not a happy idea and the donkey protested with braying which could be heard half a mile. For some unearthly reason my father seemed to enjoy this, or perhaps he enjoyed the effect it had on other people.

We also kept bees. The blizzard of 1888, which is still spoken of in New England as the Great Blizzard, destroyed half the hives. It became my settled conviction that it did not destroy enough. There was no one on the place who handled bees, so when a hive swarmed, as it seemed to me one was always doing, a frantic search was made for the bee expert. Having seen this hiving done many times, I once in a rash moment when I was older volunteered to do it myself. Swathed in veils and thick garments, I essayed the task. Nervousness or some peculiar lack of technique on my part communicated itself to the highly sensitive and overcritical bees, and to make matters worse, when the branch on which they were settled was half sawed through, it broke. The infuriated bees got inside my veil and moreover stung through some supposedly impenetrable stockings. I needed both hands to complete my task and for five minutes I was at their mercy. Finally I got them into the hive and the work done, but worse than the stings of the bees was the sight of my father, seen out of the corner of my eye, actually rolling on the ground with laughter, but at a safe distance. After all, they were his bees, as I pointed out with bitterness and emphasis, and I was doing this for him and it wasn't a matter to be laughed about. I deeply regret to say that at my protest he laughed all the harder. It was his characteristic love of a practical joke. One of his granddaughters has declared, very wrongly of course, that no Moody ever laughs at anything unless blood is drawn. But the fact remains that, while the tenderest-hearted man in the world, he could enjoy laughing at something the victim did not consider so excruciatingly funny. On the other hand I never knew him to fail to take a joke, and he enjoyed jokes upon himself as much as those on anyone else.

We could have bought all the honey our household used at a fraction of the cost and worry, but it would not have been half as much fun. I do not think anyone "told" the bees that December day when my father died, but a year or two later there were none left. What became of them, whether my mother disposed of them or they just disappeared, no one knows.

Jokes upon himself he even relished. Many times he told of one experience. He had a neighbor who stammered badly. Seeing him drawing a load of gravel on one occasion, he suggested playfully, knowing what the answer would be, that it would be a very generous thing to take the gravel to our yard and dump it where it was needed. The stutterer left his load of gravel, with typical Yankee deliberation approached my father's carriage, probably putting his foot on the hub of the wheel and his elbow on the tire, and proceeded.

He had been thinking, he said, of something my father could do which would completely eclipse anything he had done and would make the town talk from one end to the other in amazement. But he started to turn away with the remark that it was no use saying anything about it, for it was impossible. This, of course, piqued my father, but the neighbor was obdurate and would only say that it was no use, it could n't be done. To my father a challenge of this sort was like blood to a man-eating tiger. The contest went on all day, Father deliberately driving by the place where the farmer was working. The more insistent Father became, the more coy grew the holder of the secret. Mr. Sankey passed and was drawn in, the farmer declaring that it was true for Sankey too. The build-up was perfect. At last, after long discussion and pledges of secrecy, after reaffirmations of the impossibility of the attempt and renewals of the pledge of secrecy, the farmer finally was weakening in response to one last request. After a long preamble of its impossibility and secrecy he said, "I-i-it's to m-m-m-mind your own bu-bu-business!"

The hen yards were surrounded by vegetable gardens. Now a good-sized family can be comfortably provided for from a garden plot well tended and not more than one hundred feet square. I hope the size of our family will not be judged by the fact that we usually had four acres at least under cultivation. Father liked to see things grow. We could have gone into market gardening had we chosen. An asparagus patch was maintained which could have fed a hundred, and the same thing was true of the strawberry bed. And as he could n't bear to see things wasted, these strawberries would be picked and the asparagus cut and given away. To this end he usually drove about in gardening time in the most uncomfortable of express wagons and dispensed these at back doors over a radius of three or four miles. As most of this work was done by hired labor and the garden truck was given away, there was nothing in it but fun. And not much of that for me. I said most of the work was done by hired labor. Not all. Mindful of his own barefooted youth, Father would be visited now and again by a theory that I ought to get closer to the soil, so he would ordain that I put in an hour or two hours a day weeding, and add to this order, which *was* an order, his powers of persuasion that I should do it barefooted. This I would not do. Usually, as the summer wore on, he would forget about this established discipline and it would be overlooked till the following spring. But not always. He overheard me once say, as I marched off for the garden, that he had one of his work fits on, but that he would recover. He chuckled away and, that year, was a long time forgetting the discipline, and I had cause to regret my hasty words.

What most characterized him when he was home was a sort of camaraderie. I do not know a word which indicates the opposite of what the younger generation describe as a "stuffed shirt." If I did, I should use that in describing my father. I once heard a man say that Vermonters do not think they are as good as you are. They think you are as good as they are. There is a difference and it is not so subtle.

That describes my father in his family relations and of course it is only in these that I write of him. He was a stout and bearded Peter Pan, a boy who never grew up, when he was on vacation. He shamefacedly did things he knew he would be lovingly scolded for doing. But he had a perfectly wonderful time both doing them and defending himself for doing them. And he actually seemed to enjoy the remonstrances of the family and particularly those of my mother, who was, before everything else, practical and orderly.

Once, as a result of his stay in Ireland in 1892, he even purchased a jaunting car which he brought back to Northfield. It was as highly unsuitable to the roads about Northfield as it was exotic in appearance. Far too heavy for the normal horse, it was seldom used, but so strongly and ruggedly built that it surely has never worn out. It was just one of his hobbies in which he soon lost interest. You could never tell where he would break out next. Once he brought back a weight-lifting machine, an early, unscientific, and very clumsy contraption on which it was vainly supposed that valuable exercise could be obtained. It was of iron and indestructible, and its sole function was to be in the way and collect dust.

II

IN THE HOME

IF he liked to raise hens and vegetables on a large scale it was because he liked to do everything on a large scale. On one occasion he became aware, or thought he did, that the china in the house was inadequate. He placed so large an order that barrels of it arrived and we have some of it still. In the same manner his attention was once caught by some Oriental rugs. They were good rugs and he apparently could n't decide which he liked best, so he bought them all and we could have gone into the retail rug business. We had enough rugs.

If his taste was not cultivated highly along these lines it was nevertheless good and he liked harmony in a room. When he could not find some things, such as tables or chairs, to his taste he had them made. He preferred his midmorning cup of tea in one particular cup and was unexpected and more or less unpredictable in his preferences. Extravagance annoyed him, but he was equally unappreciative of the cheap or shoddy. His surroundings made a difference to him and he was far from indifferent to them at home, however tolerant he might be of inconveniences when traveling. But the unnecessary endurance of discomfort was no Christian grace to be cultivated. He was no more an ascetic than a sybarite. And he loved good food.

On another occasion out West he saw some paintings and fully a dozen must have been shipped on, and our home and my brother's and sister's houses were equipped with oil paintings. Three still hang on the walls of my home; one of Mount Hood, one of Multnomah Falls, and another of Point Loma. Apparently he could n't be bothered selecting and he cut the Gordian knot by taking the lot. I shall be stretching the credulity of my readers, I know, but it is a fact that once he bought a gross of suspenders. He found he was short of suspenders and he could not bear to be out of anything on the one hand or, on the other, to bother to replenish his wardrobe at frequent intervals. This was n't going to happen again, and it did n't. One hundred and forty-four suspenders, large size, all white, would last a considerable number of men a considerable time. Of course long before he could wear a tenth of them the rubber in the rest had rotted. But he never ran out of suspenders again.

His neckties, the old-fashioned flat Ascot which he had made to order, he also bought by the gross, which was more understandable, for he would wear one only a few times. He bought his shoes in the same way. By reason of his build he could not buy shoes ready made, his boot being both short and wide, and he would order many pairs. His early days in the whole-sale shoe business had given him a knowledge of leather and he always enjoyed buying shoes. As he grew stout he adopted elastic-sided shoes. Once, in a misguided moment, hating the looks of them, I persuaded him to buy laced shoes. This was a very, very serious mistake, for I had to lace them and he would chuckle at my lack of appreciation of the privilege. Once he went with me to buy shoes and I remember this event vividly. I was at the impressionable age when appearance counts for a good deal and I had my own quite definite conceptions of what constituted a good shoe. So did he. Style was my criterion and leather his, and he turned up his nose impatiently and brushed aside all the shoes we were shown, selecting, he declared, the only pair made of decent leather in the shop, regardless alike of fit, style, or my feverish protest. That it was good leather was too amply demonstrated by the fact that I could never wear the wretched things out, though because I hated them so I may have spared them.

It might be inferred that Father farmed, but this would be misleading. It is true that in addition to the horses and dogs and hens he delighted in keeping pigs, in which he always took a very lively interest, and cows. He liked Jersey cows because of the richness of their milk and there were always a few on the place, but the breeding of blooded stock, either horses or cows, did not appeal to him. Once he imported some sheep, but these he soon gave to his brother. The place was not large enough for farming, consisting as it did of only some fourteen acres.

The way in which he came into possession of this place, which remained his home until he died, is interesting. His mother had a neighbor with whom there was some difficulty over a line fence, her hens getting through on the neighbor's land or vice versa. This was in 1875, and my father was resting from his campaigns in Great Britain, living with my mother, brother, and sister at his birthplace. Disputes of this sort always distressed him and his solution was short and direct. He made an offer for his neighbor's farm, impulsively and overgenerously. It was immediately accepted and the line-fence dispute was settled in this way. And because his mother's house was becoming crowded with his own family, he made this new purchase his home. This took place before I was born and I only recollect the home after it had begun to undergo the additions and changes which he was constantly making. His only home of his own up to this time had been destroyed in the Chicago fire in 1871.

Father narrowly escaped coming into possession of another farm for which this time he had no use. He had bought a small house near by which accompanied a large and assorted collection of ugly unpainted barns, I dare not say how many. It was an almost perfect eyesore. Most of these sheds were pulled down with little effort — they were ready to fall. But one of them had such sound timbers that it seemed a pity to destroy it, and Father offered it to the next-door neighbor on condition he would move it out of sight. This neighbor, frugal soul, crossed the road and sold it for twenty-five dollars to a second neighbor, who had an even worse and more extensive collection of unpainted barns and sheds, by all odds the worst or in its way the most perfect eyesore in town. Then the fun began. Learning of the disposition of the barn, Father pointed out the condition of the gift, that it should be put out of sight, and the barn was not the property of neighbor number one if he sold it to neighbor number two unless neighbor number two put it out of sight, which was not his way of treating unsightly objects. He left them as near the road as possible. Endless argument ensued on this point. Number one took the twenty-five dollars reluctantly back to number two, who refused the money and demanded the barn. Further endless argument, but Father was adamant. Finally, exasperated beyond caution, he offered number two ten thousand dollars for his place, the option to run until the following Wednesday. As values went then the place was worth perhaps twenty-five hundred. The words were hardly out of Father's mouth before cold fear assailed him. He did not know where to put his hand on ten thousand dollars. But number two, a Yankee trader, promptly reasoned that if D. L. would give ten thousand he would give twelve or fifteen, and stuck out for it. The option expired and Father gave gigantic sighs of relief. Then number two, realizing his mistake, came around the next day. It was too late. I recall him sitting on a sofa in the library lowering his price and Father sitting at his desk pretending to read his mail and refusing every offer, though the offers came down to the approximate value of the place. But it was a very narrow escape from the consequences of his impulsiveness. It was a warning, and no more impulsive offers were made after this to avoid quarrels over twenty-five dollars. But while the matter dragged along it was epic in its intensity.

The house he bought was a typical New England farmhouse of that period, and four rooms remain unchanged to this day. The year that Alaska was purchased by the government a wing was added to the north, in the upper part of which he had his own study-bedroom and bath. This addition was nicknamed Alaska, in honor of the event of that year, and highly appropriately so, for having no cellar under it at that time it was extremely cold and usually uninhabitable except in summer.

The house was connected with the barns in the accepted fashion of New England, and the place had the full complement of main barn, cow barn, sheep shed, corn house, ice house, pig pens, and chicken yards. It was ideal with its haymows for a young boy and no less so for rats, for whom it was a Utopia. In the barns my father made little or no change. He was not interested in the livestock being stabled too fancifully and he liked the rustic touch. As a boy he had worked for his neighbor now and then at haying time and he liked seeing things as he had known them. The place was surrounded by an apple orchard, never scientifically tended, and meadows, and behind it to the east low rolling hills, on one of which he is buried.

The view from this home was always a favorite with him. The house faces the west and from the small front porch there is a splendid panorama of the Connecticut River with the lower hills of New Hampshire and Vermont in the background. He particularly delighted in this view at sunset as the sun sank behind the rolling wooded slopes across the river, and, every evening when he could, he watched the fading day as long as possible. The Northfield Seminary grew and finally school property surrounded it on every side, which increased his pleasure.

His letters to the members of his family when he was away were full of references to his fondness for it, and as winter wore away and he became conscious of the return of spring they were pathetic in their expressions of genuine homesickness, and he was counting the weeks and days until he could get back, lay off his dark clothes, and give full rein to his absorbing passion for watching things grow.

Vacations have been alluded to, and of course it was on these that I saw the most of my parents. But as for vacations in the usual sense of the term, they were hardly these. For Father rose early and retreated to his upstairs study, where he worked for a time. His work usually consisted in the days when I knew him of preparing new sermons, writing outlines, and reading what related to what he was preparing his notes about. I do not believe he ever wrote out a sermon, and it is certain he never

used a written one. By the time I remember
him he was not a great reader. I do not believe
he ever wrote out a paragraph of what he was

going to say. His mind worked much too fast
for his hand; he contented himself with notes,
great sprawling words which connoted something to him but to no one else.

There hangs on my study wall a framed outline of a sermon by Henry Drummond on "The Ideal Life." Drummond wrote a highly legible, delicate, and beautiful hand, and this sermon is a model of arrangement. I remember distinctly my father showing it to me once when we were out driving. He had seen it in Drummond's hands after an address and it was such a marvelous contrast to his own scrawls that he had begged for it. It was wonderful to him, passing words, that anyone could write so clearly and beautifully and arrange his outline with such precision, the important heads in such large letters and the minor points correspondingly diminished. He had added in his own large hand two references which stood out in marked contrast to the clerkly script of his friend. He admired it greatly as a work of art and then, to my surprise, gave it to me. His own notes were strikingly different and in such large letters did he write that they would cover all four sides of folded writing paper and there would be six or eight or more of these folded into elastic bands placed in his Bible. Some of his morning must have gone into the preparation of these notes. But not the entire ante-prandial morning, for, as I have said, he would be out driving, feeding his chickens, or distributing vegetables before the family were awake or down.

In the vacation he liked to have people about him and the house would be full. Too full, I often thought as I surrendered successively one room after another to guests who were not always too fascinating to my boyish fancy, though some were welcome, like Drummond or George Adam Smith. There were also a few nieces and nephews for good measure. Dinner was in the middle of the day. It was a waste of good time to be long at supper. Supper interfered with watching the sunset over his favorite hills, and he would have moved the supper hour back to an indecently early hour had it not been for my mother's protest. Some of my dearest memories are connected with the gradual gathering about noontime in the library in anticipation of the noonday dinner. The mail would have recently come in and it was invariably large. He would sit in a huge chair he had had made on purpose, at the very desk at which I now write, the chair pushed back from the desk, his glasses on the end of his nose, opening and glancing at letter after letter. If the family and guests were gathered about, he would delight in thrusting the letter back in the envelope, flipping it at one or another with a brusque "Answer that!" If the unfortunate recipient of the letter presumed to ask what he or she was to say in answer he would playfully snort, "I gave it to *you* to answer! I don't intend to hire a dog and do the barking." He loved and used the homely colloquialisms of New England and he was full of them. Sometimes the letters demanded his attention and he was ready to give it when really needed, but he used to give the most surprising letters to people to answer. Guests, I say, came in for this for the simple reason that he treated them as members of the family. By the time I was fifteen I was alone at home as my brother and sister had married and were in homes of their own. But I never remember the house in summer being other than comparatively full.

I never remember seeing my father dictate a letter. My brother-in-law-to-be was asked to this country as his secretary, but there was a sense in which he never had a secretary. And later my brother answered many letters for him. But he himself wrote in answer to many, and many others he turned over to my mother, who, in addition to attending largely to his mail, particularly when he was away, looked after all business matters. Here again he could not be bothered. The house was hers and everything he had.

Another device of his was to turn over to members of his household requests for short articles or contributions to symposiums. These he would sign and the proceeds went to who-ever wrote them. The first money I ever earned was twenty dollars for some short article. It was necessary both to catch his ideas and at the same time to express them as he would have done. And he was merciless in his amusement if the luckless ghost writer used a two- or three-dollar word which he would not have em-ployed. One such article I wrote I remember distinctly, for in it I represented him as saying that higher criticism was less dangerous than unchristian attacks upon it. Of course all these articles were submitted to him; and I queried what I had written myself, for while it was my own immature conviction I was not certain he would subscribe to it. He pondered it for a little time thoughtfully and then replied that he would let it stand. It angered one fundamentalist friend dreadfully.

Once, when still a boy, I had to lead a Christian Endeavor meeting. Very carefully I wrote out what I was going to say and sought my father's advice. The little talk began with a quotation from Emerson. Immediately he pounced on this. It was not the quotation to which he objected. "Say," he suggested, " 'someone has said' rather than 'Emerson says.' People will think you are trying to show off." He was always himself the jury lawyer trying to get a verdict, the salesman trying to sell a bill of goods, and anything which stood between the message and the group, however beautiful in itself, was not allowed. You may search his sermons in vain for quotations. Anecdotes, yes, usually personal ones in his own experience; Biblical quotations, yes, but never what would be called literary ones, the type that so appeals to many finished and also unfinished speakers.

This may have been due to his poor verbal memory. I once heard him say that often as he had used the Lord's Prayer, he never dared use it without the actual words before him. Apt phrases impressed him, I know. We found among some papers of his the words of Rudyard Kipling in one of his poems: —

> Help me to need no aid from men
> That I may help such men as need.

He was very much interested in Rudyard Kipling, who for a time was a relatively near neighbor when he lived in Brattleboro, which was twelve miles distant. I, like all boys of that age at that time, was an admirer of Kipling, whom we sometimes saw driving through Northfield, and Father several times urged me to write inviting Kipling to lunch, a suggestion we never carried out, having heard perhaps exaggerated rumors of a certain aloofness of Kipling's. I have always regretted that I did not at least extend the invitation. I learned after it was too late that they had many friends in common in Vermont and I think they would have appreciated each other. For my father was always interested in people who did things, however far removed from his own line of activity.

Once, when we were staying at the Murray Hill Hotel, I pointed out Richard Croker. Father immediately went up and introduced himself and had a ten- or fifteen-minute talk. When he rejoined me I asked what in the world he had to talk to Richard Croker about. This was in the days of Croker's power. He replied he had asked Croker to use his influence against a bill in the New York Legislature providing for the opening of theatres on Sunday. Croker was noncommittal and I have often wondered since whether it was really Father's interest in the defeat of this bill, which he deplored, as much as it was to find a pretext for meeting the great Tammany chieftain which prompted him; for he had, as I have said, a veiled admiration for men who came to the top in almost any line of activity. He certainly never attended a prize fight, for he frowned upon this sport, but when the papers recorded the defeat of John L. Sullivan by Corbett, he repeatedly referred to the matter, expressing his sympathy for one, long the champion, who had been overthrown. I think he felt genuinely sorry for the famous old John L.

During a short stay in Portland, Maine, when William Jennings Bryan on his first campaign came to that city, sitting at the open window of his hotel room, my father heard him. While he revolted strongly from all Bryan's policies and platform, he was immensely impressed by the Boy Orator's eloquence and persuasiveness and obvious sincerity, and remarked that it was fortunate he did not hear him more often. He redoubled his own personal efforts then in behalf of McKinley without actually taking the stump, and it was at this time he read a lecture to one of his associates who remarked that, his citizenship being in Heaven, he was not going to vote. No matter where my father was he personally returned home to vote, and the exercise of the franchise he considered a Christian duty, as well as to be informed on all political matters. He was a Republican all his days, to the deep disgust of some of his prohibitionist friends who felt he might have been a tower of strength to their party. But, while a rigid teetotaler himself, he felt the control of liquor was a state or local matter and not a federal one; and I have heard him defend his position by saying often that no law was stronger than the local sentiment. Local option was, in his view, the only way to handle the liquor question. He had among his friends anti-tobacconists, teetotalers, and one with whom secret societies had become an obsession. He tolerated these people, feeling that while they meant well they were getting the cart before the horse and letting their phobias run away with them. Fanatics always repelled him, for he was the embodiment of common sense.

Some can recall how on one occasion a

movement was launched at Northfield, The Northfield Emergency Missionary Fund, to supplement the work of the Mission Boards. He was not on hand to quash it before it got started. But when it came to his attention, his action was direct. He sent for all the hotheads and enthusiasts who had started the move. They came in the evening and were fed ice cream. He was unusually silent. After the refreshments he seized a lamp (we had no electricity) and led the now bewildered group into another room. It was a long time before they came out, chastened and subdued. On occasions like this he could be very grim. The Kingdom of God was sacred to him and was not advanced by nonsense, however sanctified, or solemn hocus-pocus. He often affirmed that dignity was never mentioned as one of the fruits of the spirit. In his judgment a man who had to stand on his dignity must be a very short man indeed to need so cumbersome a soapbox. With all extremes, sensationalism, or pomposity he had scant sympathy.

Guests came to this simple New England

farmhouse. I remember John B. Gough and General O. O. Howard and C. C. Coffin, whose books in that day had a wide public. Joseph Parker came too, but he was under a contract not to speak and he could only say a word to the students who serenaded him. Once when he was Governor General of Canada, the Earl of Aberdeen, whom Father had known in Scotland, came with the Countess and his family and a considerable number of secretaries and aides, appropriate for so conspicuous a position. I suspect my mother's influence in having the party steered to the hotel. Father, hospitable soul, was quite capable of saying, "Come and stay with me." Earls were uncommon in Northfield and the proper form of address a matter of worry. One man at the hotel called the Governor General "Mr. Earl," and felt quite pleased at this democratic solution.

As a gesture of hospitality the party were invited to the house for breakfast. After family prayers, which wisely followed breakfast (no tantalizing of a hungry family by the smell of coffee and bacon while devotions were going on for Father!), we adjourned to the front porch. There the young daughter of the family, an ardent entomologist, though aged about ten, saw in the meadow opposite some butterflies. She was equipped with a butterfly net. But the grass was waist-high and soaking wet with dew and her little ladyship could not be allowed to wet her feet. Now good timothy ready for the teeth of the mower is not treated disrespectfully, and any country youth knows enough to keep out of it. Imagine then my surprise at being instructed, dressed in my Sunday best as I was, to take that net and capture some specimens. With futility and embarrassment I chased those wretched butterflies all over that lot. I never caught one, but did catch the best drenching from the heavy dew. It made a deep impression on me of the sanctity of hospitality, for even good timothy on the verge of mowing might be trampled down with impunity in the interest of a guest. Nothing was too good.

III

FATHER AND MOTHER

IF in retrospect our home seemed so ideal, the secret was my mother. My father's admiration for her was as boundless as his love. To the day of his death, I believe, he never ceased to wonder at two things — the use God had made of him despite what he considered his handicaps, and the miracle of having won the love of a woman he considered so completely his superior, with such a different temperament and background. In his judgment it was a reversal of King Cophetua and the beggar maidén. My mother had seen in him in his raw youth what others came to see, and her confidence in him and her willingness to share his highly uncertain future gave him courage.

My mother's father was a shipbuilder by profession, a Frenchman of Huguenot blood who came to England and there met and married my grandmother. After business reverses in England and a serious fall from the scaffolding of his shipyard which impaired his health,

he brought his three daughters and a son to Chicago in 1849, when my mother was six years old. The financial means of the Revells were small, and as soon as she received sufficient education my mother became a teacher.

My father met her when she was twelve and when she was seventeen they became engaged, and two years later, in 1862, they were married, he meanwhile having given up business to devote himself to his Sunday School and other activities. Two statements made by my father seem inconsistent — one that they met in a Baptist Sunday School where they both taught, the other that they met when she was twelve. Yet both statements may be correct.

All girlhood pictures of my mother represent her as beautiful and I, who remember her only in early middle life when youthful beauty had matured into womanly charm, think of her as one of the most beautiful women I have ever seen. Her hair was iron gray at forty, snow white at sixty when she died. She had the reserve which we usually refer to as British and a quiet dignity which never deserted her, but her real strength of character was concealed under her shyness and graciousness. I never remember seeing her excited or flustered or anything but mistress of herself and the situation. She was self-disciplined to an unusual degree. In the last two years of her life she learned to write with her left hand, neuritis having made the use of her right hand difficult, and she attained proficiency with it.

So retiring and shy was she by nature that life would have been intolerable to her had she not been so completely wrapped up and absorbed in her love for her husband and conscious of his own deep and wondering love for her. She suffered as a young woman from asthma and all her life was subject to intense headaches, but she never allowed her health to interfere in any way with the discharge of her duties. My father's robust health and tireless energy were in striking contrast, but with chivalrous care he endeavored to shield her.

No two people were ever more in contrast in other matters than health. He was impulsive, outspoken, dominant, informal, and with little education at the time they met. She was intensely conventional and conservative, far better educated, fond of reading, with a discriminating taste, and self-effacing to the last degree. She was not one to make confidences or invite them. He was forever brushing over barriers. Yet they presented one common front to the world. He said of her that she was the only one in their thirty-seven years of married life who never tried to hold him back from anything he wanted to do and was always in sympathy with every new venture.

If they presented a common front to the world, it was even more the case at home. It would have been the rankest treason to have tried to secure the consent of one alone. It was invariably "See what Father says" — "See what Mother says." Yet often if we had been able to get their individual opinions on certain matters I am sure they would have been different.

The wives of so many men in public life love the limelight. My mother hated it. She was happiest in her home, where she loved to pursue housewifely tasks, putting up preserves, making raspberry vinegar or ginger beer from a recipe brought from England, driving about among those who depended upon her, writing letters and entertaining my father's friends. For, quite apart from house guests, my father loved to have in groups after the evening meetings at Northfield, twenty or thirty at a time. Watermelons or ice cream would be served. During the student conferences delegations would come from the colleges. In August it would be speakers or others to whom he wished to pay some attention. Over all this my mother presided self-effacingly and efficiently.

It is doubtful if anything distressed my father more than idleness, and not only was he busy but he wanted others busy too. He was fond of saying, "The devil tempts most men, but a lazy man tempts the devil." The work in the garden which he sporadically ordained for me was not enough. During long summer afternoons I played host-coachman to visitors, particularly to those from abroad, and drove and drove about the countryside through the wooded roads, of which Northfield in those days offered so many. It was a privilege on the whole, I suppose, but tennis courts did look inviting, though I seldom got onto one. Instead I listened to discussions on theology from men who often irritated me by their indifference to the beauties of a brook or the effect of dappled sunlight through waving branches across a winding road.

But my real responsibility was for the ice cream which we made in too great bulk for the hordes who would be invited in after the evening service. In these effeminate days when all you do is to turn a switch on the electric refrigerator, it is no task, but then it was. You got the ice out of the cool, sun-dusted recesses of the ice house, washed it off, broke it up, and churned and churned. Once I remember I learned to my disgust that the group which was coming that night was one of which I disapproved. There was a girl in this group who I thought had "high-hatted" me. I spent almost the entire day freezing, packing, and repacking. I was carrying on experiments in the nature of refrigeration and I got satisfactory results. When the hour arrived that column of ice cream was with difficulty dislodged from the freezer and it was frozen so solidly that it could not be cut. My father worked away on the resistant mass. He could chip it but he could not cut it. He called for heavier knives, with no better results. Finally containers of boiling water were brought in and the knives heated in these. Still with little or no result. My father was looking more and more baffled, I remaining as innocent-looking as I could. I never enjoyed ice cream more, though I do not recall getting any, but I had my reward for my day's toil in the politely expectant faces of the waiting guests. I hoped, of course, that such expertness would indicate I was capable of higher things. I am sure I have never done anything else so well, but alas, the artist frequently finds himself far in advance of his day. My efforts were not appreciated.

Another boyhood task was keeping a bushel basket filled with apples at the entrance of our drive. The capacity for apples among attendants at the Conferences was amazing. It even exceeded their capacity, also amazing to a boy, for attending meetings. Two or three times a day this basket had to be replenished. The apples, of course, were given away and people took them with the same horrid avidity with which they will take anything that is free. To this day I meet people who remember those apples. But they never knew the bitterness of heart with which that seemingly bottomless basket was repeatedly filled.

When away from Northfield my mother was equally busy making a home-away-from-home for Father, shielding him as far as she could from interruptions and from bores and cranks, always in abundance, answering when possible his letters, attending to his clothes, supplying money, paying bills, and doing all in her power to set him free for the work he was doing and in which she took the greatest pride and interest. But sit on the platform or be in the least degree conspicuous? Not she! If she took a pride, as she must have, in being consulted by my father, she not only concealed it but concealed as far as possible his actual dependence upon her judgment. She exercised her great and wise influence from the background and the farther back it was the happier she felt. Only the closest and oldest of his associates knew the extent to which he leaned upon her. She did not intend they should.

Mother took over entirely the matter of finance. Father never in my time had a bank account or wrote a check. It was she who paid every bill, including those for his harmless if not inexpensive hobbies, sent us children money when it was needed, and paid the taxes and looked after the needy. Whenever Father went off on a trip it was she who furnished the money. No human being could have been more indifferent to it than he was. Yet he endeavored to inculcate in his children a sense of the value of money. His own extreme poverty as a young man was a background. I have heard him tell of sliding on the ice in his bare feet because shoes and stockings were luxuries reserved for Sunday, and I have also heard him tell of taking the snow out from the cracks of his bare feet after sliding on the ice.

My mother had a delightful sense of humor and she and my father enjoyed rallying each other gently. And while she was never caustic or unkind she could enlighten her conversation and clarify her views with a gentle sarcasm which we both enjoyed and feared.

Her reading voice was very lovely and some of my pleasantest recollections are of hearing her read aloud. I do not know whether *Henry Esmond* is as wonderful as it seems to me, or whether my partiality towards it is connected with the conditions under which I made its acquaintance. During my freshman year in college I had the measles, and during my convalescence I was not allowed to use my eyes. Mother was in Florida with Father at the time and on learning of my illness took the first train for New Haven, and there she climbed the many flights to my room in old Pierson and we followed the adventures of *Henry*. Dr. Henry van Dyke had recommended it the previous summer as, along with *Lorna Doone* and *Romola*, one of the three great historical novels.

My mother was, in point of time as well as importance, my first Bible teacher. During my boyhood, particularly on Sunday afternoons,

I was set to memorize certain Psalms and passages from the Gospels. The value of this I did not at the time appreciate to the full and it was accomplished with persistence on her part, gentle but firm, and much ill-advised and entirely futile opposition on my own. She would drop comments on the passages and elucidate them, and now, when I am past middle age, there are passages which recall her. Since those far-off days I have studied under some well-known and highly learned scholars of the Old and the New Testament, here and abroad, but to none do I feel as indebted as I do to her for whatever understanding I may have. And now I am grateful for the memorizing.

It is Lady Asquith who said of her own sister that she was a saint and being a saint was "influenceable." It is a clumsy word, but one descriptive of my mother. Brought up a Baptist, she remained one at heart, though she loyally joined the Congregational Church with my father. A little while before her death, being impressed by a sermon on baptism by F. W. Robertson of Brighton, under whose spell I had fallen, I read it to her. She listened intently but volunteered no comment. When pressed for what she thought of it she replied, "It is well expressed and plausible, but it does not voice my feelings in the matter of baptism." That was that!

On one occasion she undertook to study Latin grammar for no other reason than to help and encourage me, who even at an early age was displaying marked linguistic inaptitude. She was never too busy amid all her tasks to help me with my studies, and her own brief experience as a schoolteacher, added to her clear mind, enabled her to do it extremely well, with, I confess I must add, inexhaustible patience. French, which was her father's native language, she relearned. She mastered anything which challenged her, as she did in the end the use of her left hand. My father's reliance upon her judgment, in some respects much keener than his, was complete. She was his complement in so many ways and at all times a balance wheel. But she never allowed this to be evident. In all his early meetings she helped in the inquiry room, but I do not recall her doing it in the years when I was observant and I cannot imagine it as other than distasteful to her with her instinctive reserve. I always found it easier to confess any shortcomings to my father than to her, and easier, too, to confide in him. She had few intimates. I doubt indeed if she had any apart from my father. One Englishwoman whom she seldom saw was closer to her, I think, than anyone else.

I never knew anyone more free from vindictiveness. But there was one thing she never did or would forgive, and that was anything in the nature of a disloyalty to my father. He was taken advantage of often. He learned himself that there were certain people he could not trust and some with whom he ceased to work accused him of betraying friends. It was not that in reality. It was the feeling on his part that they had been untrue to the centre of his loyalties and he could not work with people he did not trust. But my mother would not mention such people. They fell at once into the limbo of the unthought of. Her affection and admiration for my father were such that disloyalty to him was the unpardonable sin in her eyes, unforgivable, unforgettable, and above all unmentionable. The gentlest and kindest and most thoughtful of women, here she was implacable.

My father also had few intimates. I very seldom heard him call anyone by his first name beyond the family and, except for some old neighbors and his brother, I never heard him called "Dwight" by his contemporaries. He dropped handles. Ira Sankey was always "Sankey" to him. Perhaps the man who entered deepest of his generation into his affection and confidence was Henry M. Moore of Boston. Mr. Moore used to reply, when asked his business, "My business is to preach the Gospel, but I sell hats to make a living." Those who knew Father best realized this most. Now and again I meet someone who tells me he knew my father intimately. And this means to me that he knew him very slightly. He did disarm those he met and drew them to him, but I am persuaded that beyond a certain point nobody went except my mother. He was an open book to her.

When old friends came to the house at the time of Father's funeral, they were taken in to see her. No matter in what frame of mind they entered the room, they came out comforted and strengthened. She, whose loss was greater than their own, whose whole life was so violently disarranged, had strength for her own needs and enough to spare for others. But it was soon evident that life was over for her. For us, her children, she was content to linger, but the incentive was gone, the mainspring broken. She never allowed us to see her sense of loss. She went placidly on with what was left of her round of duties, her thoughtful kindnesses, her provision for the family, her interest in her grandchildren. But it was not the same.

Looking back, I feel as we all felt while they were together, that the keen edge of appreciation and affection for each other was never dulled. My father was as solicitous of and for her as he must have been as a bridegroom, and perhaps even more so, for I am sure he grew more considerate under her unfailing example. It was chivalry of the rarest type. I never remember his being more put out with me than once when I had caused her worry by being out too late. He had worried too, but that did not matter. I had caused her worry, and he was outspoken in the matter.

To my mother I am very sure belongs the credit of having, by precept and example, made my father what he was in one respect, the most courteous man I ever knew. He did not, I admit, draw out chairs for ladies at the table or excel in passing afternoon teacups. All this side of life was missing in his early bringing-up. But in setting people at their ease, in avoiding the hurting of feelings, in all the finer sensibilities, he was and remains my ideal. He has been accused of being brusque. Direct he certainly was. The Czar who drew a straight line between Moscow and St. Petersburg and said, "Build the railroad there," was one he could understand. He never wasted words or motions, but went to his goal in the shortest, most direct way. I grant he did not say, "Please hold this horse for me," but "Hold this horse." And he might gather up the reins and drive off afterwards without a long speech of acknowledgment and admission of an over-burdening sense of obligation. But you knew that he would have held the horse for you if you had asked it, and expected no bouquets for the great favor he had conferred. I was with him in the homes of some of the donors to the Schools, wealthy people. He was at ease and everyone else was as much so as they were at our own broad table. Well I remember a curtain lecture I received in Paris when I had replied with directness to an inquiry as to how I liked Paris by an American living there. My defense was that I felt I should tell the truth. I hated it. It was pointed out to me quite inescapably that this was not a moral matter but one in the field of good breeding, and that I need not have been either so categorical or so sweeping and that I might at least have mentioned those aspects of the French capital that I did like.

In all this it is easy to see my mother's hand.

MY FATHER

The New Englander is apt not only to be blunt but to pride himself on it. And the gentle influence of my mother could not fail to be a corrective. So many of the early stories of my father show a directness of approach that they seem unreal to me. I do not doubt their truth. I only say I did not so know him, and in the last third of his life when alone I remember him the certain influence of my mother must be held accountable. Deep as his convictions were I never knew him to be as outspoken about them or as insistent upon them with those who did not share them as he has been represented in passages describing his early days. I repeat that I do not deny that he was dominant in this way. I only affirm that this is not how I remember him and I think my mother is accountable.

He loved to drive with her, and with her alone he drove sanely and with care. Now and again the two of them would drive off for a few days, through the quiet woods of Vermont or New Hampshire, going where fancy led them, having as it were a renewed honey-moon. Once, on one of these occasions, spending a Sunday in rest, he wired for me to join them. In church that day he was recognized, and while he would have preferred to worship in a pew he was haled to the pulpit and had to preach. I never knew him to decline such invitations, though they were as unwelcome as they were unsought. It was on this particular trip that they suddenly left a small inn of which they had heard much and which was one of the goals of the trip. Father would say nothing about it. Mother laughingly confided that Father could not stand it, as the noisy way one of the guests had eaten had gotten on his nerves. It amused her immensely.

It is thus, driving together in the cool of the evening in the then unmotor-ridden roads of the countryside they both loved, — "Lover's Retreat," the "Gulf Road," or the "Long Square," — that I like best to recall them. For the most part they rode in silence, I imagine, for such was the understanding and sympathy between them that they needed no words. I have never seen anything more idyllic, nor do I believe two people, young or old, were ever more completely wrapped up in each other.

IV

IN THE FAMILY

FAMILY ties were always strong with my father. This feeling was early ingrained in him. When his own father died and creditors came in, his mother was left with seven children all young and twins were born to her soon after. Neighbors advised against trying to hold the family together, but she did, and with the help of the second son, George, to whom my father was always deeply attached, she won out. The children early learned both to work and to go without things. While my father left home at seventeen he seems to have been a pretty constant correspondent, and the hold his mother had over him was very great. She was a Unitarian, and prior to my father's leaving home he attended that church. Later she affiliated herself with the Congregational Church as did her son George. He became a deacon.

MY FATHER

I remember my grandmother only as a very old lady and a good deal of a matriarch. She lived till she died in the home where the children had been born. Her long grim struggle with poverty as she brought up her fatherless brood had ingrained in her habits of thrift and economy which persisted long after the need. It was my father's constant effort to ameliorate her living conditions, an effort against which she silently struggled. He found her drinking tea out of a marmalade jar, quite unnecessarily, and to correct this gave her china which she stubbornly refused to employ, on which he gave her more. Finally a compromise was reached when another son gave her a very ugly but unbreakable metal cup and saucer. These she used. But so completely the Puritan was she and so deep-seated the lifelong habits that it used to seem to us, her grandchildren, that she preferred to be uncomfortable and found a degree of virtue in it. I do not know, but I suspect that when my father added a sunny living room to her side of the house he did it over her protest.

We children were always given to understand that we should go to see her often. She never made any fuss over us. There was no cookie jar nor any sweets to reward good grandchildren and she seemed to be afraid of spoiling us, for she was certainly never remarkably demonstrative and, I always felt, suffered our filial kisses with a sort of grim resignation. The morning she died, when it became evident that the end was not far away, I was despatched in a sleigh to fetch my brother living five miles away. On returning we were apprised that the end had come by Father, walking down to meet us between piles of snow — with tears streaming down his face but smiling radiantly.

At her funeral he rose in the pew where he was sitting and paid a tribute to her, bringing out with unconscious but consummate artistry word sketches of that early struggle at home. He was in tears again as he did it, yet as he described the punishments she inflicted in her desire to bring up her children aright he was so graphic that ripples of laughter swept the audience. It was the most unusual and in a sense triumphant sort of funeral that I ever attended.

Having prospered more than his brothers had, it was always on his mind to help where

he could, and yet he was wise in the aid he gave. He did what he could to assist in the education of his numerous nephews and nieces, not only his own but my mother's as well. He was not afraid of nepotism and found places in the work connected with the Schools for one and another of them.

With his own children he was, as I have said, an ideal companion and on the whole a wise guide. He was, I believe, torn between two desires, one to see that we had the advantages he lacked, — education and travel and books, — the other to see that we were not deprived of the advantages of going without, the benefits of certain lacks. It will be recognized that these two ambitions are hard to reconcile.

Having himself the toughest of physiques, he was rarely if ever ill. I only remember his being housed with a cold once, and then I recall more vividly his dreadful impatience at being housed than anything else. He was n't equipped by nature to be a good invalid. One Christmas vacation when I was suffering from an attack of undiagnosed jaundice and acutely desirous only of being let alone, he could not understand why I did not want to be out in the air skating or coasting and worried himself and me in anxiety to see me doing something. Once when I was ill in a nursing home in England he was dreadfully concerned, though I was not in any danger, and he was coming to see me all the time, looking for momentary improvement and never failing to place his heavy hand on my forehead. His hand was little lighter than a dictionary, but it was more than endurable, for all you felt was the weight of affection. I have been told that once he perched on the side of a sickbed and broke it down. In the language of New England, he was not handy about a sickroom.

He remembered birthdays and wrote or telegraphed when away from home, no matter how busy he might be, and as might be imagined he delighted to give presents. But he was a hard man to give presents to, for his wants were so few. Christmas was always a joy to him, for it gave him an excuse to exercise his generosity. He delighted to give his children trips on which he would have gladly gone himself if time permitted. He sent my sister to Norway, my brother to Alaska, and contemplated a trip for me on completion of college, which I should have taken had he lived.

Only a boy who has longed for a bicycle in that motorless age can understand just how much I was obsessed by the desire to have one. While this ambition was at its height I ran across a paper edition of his sermons. One was on prayer. In it he said that if a child of his wanted something, he would prefer to be asked for it once and not nagged. This extract I cut out, prefaced it by the statement that I wanted a bicycle, then mentioned the day some weeks hence of my birthday, and remarked that such was my faith that I was thanking him in advance for it. There was no acknowledgment. But a little later he invited me to spend Easter vacation with him in Richmond, where he was preaching. I went. Neither of us alluded to the bicycle. Wild horses would not have dragged a reference from me. My birthday fell in this period, but no reference was made to it. But on my return I found the bicycle awaiting me at home. I am under the impression that had I been so indiscreet as to allude to it I might have defeated my own ends.

Four years later, on my nineteenth birthday, I received a telegram from him. "Thank God for the past nineteen years. The —— house is your birthday present." And the house he presented me with was a dwelling in Northfield which he and my mother owned, and which remained in my possession until long after I left Northfield. On another occasion when I was younger he presented me with a driving horse, a granddaughter of his own favorite Nellie Gray. This was to replace the pony which I had by this time outgrown.

His satisfaction in doing things of this sort was always great. His gifts, whatever they were, afforded him more satisfaction than they did the recipient, whatever they meant to the recipient. He seems to me in retrospect the most generous man I ever knew, taking more delight in giving than anyone else I ever met.

When his grandchildren arrived, his delight knew no bounds. The most grotesque things he proudly bore off to them — an unusually large cabbage on one occasion to an unweaned infant. When they were older and able to be about he was seldom without one on his drives around town. His firm prejudice against being photographed broke down completely and his picture was taken again and again with the three grandchildren he lived to see — with them and with their own parents and with his own mother. On one of his drives a granddaughter went to sleep — he would not let her be disturbed as she rested on his arm. He drove into the yard, had the horse unharnessed, and waited until she woke, meanwhile utilizing the time for a nap himself. He wrote them delicious nonsense letters when away from home, making all sorts of plans for what they would do when summer came. When his own children were young he was too often away from home or too busy to extract from them all the pleasure he did from his grandchildren. He reaffirmed repeatedly what many grandparents have discovered, that grandchildren have all the endearing qualities of one's own children minus the care and responsibility, and it is safe to presume that had he lived he would have taken an impish delight in overriding parental authority and had a riotous time just plain spoiling his grandchildren, and enjoying immensely remonstrances for so doing.

One incident of my own childhood casts more light on his essential character than anything else I know. When I was quite young, a crony of mine had come over with the maid in their home to see the maids in our kitchen. I discovered him and was visiting with him in the kitchen when Father had occasion to pass through. Seeing me up past my bedtime, he told me to go to bed. I interpreted this to mean that I was to go when my little friend had left and continued talking to him, with no thought of challenge to parental authority. A few minutes later he found me still there and this time left no doubt in my mind that this was not, as they say in the army, a command of expectation, but a command of execution. This time I retreated immediately and in tears, for it was an almost unheard-of thing that he should speak with such directness or give an order unaccompanied by a smile. But I had barely gotten into my little bed before he was kneeling beside it in tears and seeking my forgiveness for having spoken so harshly. He never, he said, intended to speak crossly to one of his children.

Half a century must have passed since then and while it is not the earliest of my recollections I think it is the most vivid, and I can still see that room in twilight and that large bearded figure with the great shoulders bowed above me, and hear the broken voice and the tenderness in it. I like best to think of him that way. Before then and after I saw him holding the attention of thousands of people, but asking the forgiveness of his unconsciously disobedient little boy for having spoken harshly seemed to me then and seems now a finer and a greater thing, and to it I owe more than I owe to any of his sermons. For to this I am indebted for an understanding of the meaning of the Fatherhood of God, and a belief in the love of God had its beginnings that night in my childish mind.

V

COLLEGE CONTACTS

FATHER's interest in my departure for college and my experience with examinations could not have been greater. My schooling, owing to four winters spent with my parents away from home where I could not attend school, had been so interrupted that I got off to a bad start, and when regular work began I was handicapped. Normally I should not have gone to college until a year later than I did, and cutting off a year of preparation entailed much application and night after night I was ordered to put out the light and go to bed. When word was received that I had passed enough subjects to be admitted to Yale, I think Father's satisfaction was fully as great as my own.

The morning I left for my first absence from home, he drove me to the station. He was very quiet and had unusually little to say. To my surprise he did not ask me to observe some of the Puritan traditions we had kept, such as no theatre-going, or card playing, or traveling on Sunday, or dancing or smoking. He did say he hoped I would not smoke, but he did not lay it down as a request and far less as a command. But he revealed that he was thinking a great deal by a confidence he made and made with a certain degree of embarrassment and diffidence. He had been praying, he said, that God would use me to bring into the Kingdom all my classmates. The corner of the road, nearing the station, where he said this stands out in my memory. It is painful to make the confession that his confidence was so misplaced. Later he was delighted that the class, according to an old custom of those days, elected me one of its four deacons, charged with the religious life of the class, and he sent a message of congratulation.

During my brother's stay at Yale my father had been invited every year to be one of the college preachers, and he had accepted. After my brother's graduation he declined invitations as they interfered with his schedule. But when I entered college, the invitations still being extended, he accepted again. My freshman year I remember being morbidly anxious that he should do well. In those days it was a serious misdemeanor to exceed the time of the service. The remark that "no souls are saved after twenty minutes" is said to have originated at Battell Chapel. Father preached for nearly half an hour over the time, but there was no shuffling of feet. I suffered so acutely that I was ill the rest of the afternoon with nervous indigestion. Yet the fact that he was forgiven was evidenced by the largest crowd I had seen at the evening service, which differed from that of the morning in that it was not compulsory. Twice as many came to the old assembly room of the Dwight Hall of those days as could get in.

The following year he was invited in April. The preacher on the previous Sunday was George Adam Smith, Lyman Beecher lecturer for that year. The authorities asked Professor

Smith to speak for three nights following the Sunday, as he was spending the week there delivering the Beecher lectures. My father was invited to come ahead of time and speak the remaining three nights. My recollection is that he spent the week there, for he heard Professor Smith's lectures, or some of them, and heard some of his addresses to the students. By the lectures he was not impressed. The world knows those lectures as *Modern Criticism and the Preaching of the Old Testament*. It was for some of the things said in these lectures that the attempt was made to try Professor Smith afterwards by the conservatives of the Free Church of Scotland. My father did not hear all the lectures, but nothing he did hear offended him and he remarked to me that he did not see why people objected to them. It was after this that he invited Professor Smith to Northfield and renewed an acquaintance made years before. He was very deeply impressed by Smith's sermons and felt it a shame that one who could preach so compellingly was not relieved of every other duty and set free for preaching, particularly to young men; and it was in this connection that the oft-quoted remark was made that it was a pity to waste time telling people there were two Isaiahs when so many people did not know there was one.

Sometimes during my first two years in college Father would run down to New Haven for overnight. On one occasion I remember he came accompanied by my mother and my brother-in-law. In the corridor outside my room he picked up a playing card from the floor. This my brother-in-law, at my father's instance, slipped under the writing pad of my desk when I was not looking. My father, wandering about the room, pulled out the card. Of course I had known nothing of it and began on a series of explanations as to how it got there, till I suddenly caught the twinkle in his eye.

He wired me once that he would spend a night in New Haven and to arrange with the city Y.M.C.A. to put on a service. There was no organization worthy of the name at that time in New Haven, a few rooms being occu-

pied in Chapel Street and run by a very nonde-
script committee. I met the committee and put
the matter up to them. On my father's arrival
we found they had secured a small church in
a square on the outskirts of the town and ad-
vertised it by a placard outside. I feared this
church would not be large enough, but my
fear turned to horror, for, small as it was, it
was not half filled. On our way back that night
my father took me to task for this fiasco. I
countered by saying I had left it up to the
committee and I was told I should have had
more sense: a favorite remark of his — "You
should have had more sense." The next time he
was coming to New Haven I approached the
committee of the Y.M.C.A. in a different
mood. They were to hire, I told them, the largest theatre. They were aghast. It would cost
one hundred dollars or more. I offered to do
it myself if they would not and on this they
succumbed; more people tried to get in than
the place held and there was a large number of
college men in the audience.

In those days large groups went from Yale

to the Student Conference at Northfield, and this my father always thoroughly enjoyed. There he made the acquaintance of such men as A. A. Stagg, William Lyon Phelps, Howard Heinz, Anson Phelps Stokes, William Sloane, and Henry Coffin. To Dr. Coffin he was greatly attached and looked upon him as one of the coming leaders of the Church.

It was at Northfield during one of these Conferences that he made a celebrated break. He was preaching on Gideon and in the course of his sermon he asked what could be done with an empty pitcher and brought the point home by saying, "What would a Yale man do with an empty pitcher?" He was unprepared for the roar of laughter. For it was at this time that a very silly and fanatical paper was making all sorts of hopelessly exaggerated charges about the drinking at Yale, charges which were so groundless and absurd that they were the cause of much merriment. A few nights later at the Fourth of July celebration, the place of honor being given the Yale delegation because it was the largest, the centre of their decorations was a pitcher upside down, and Anson Phelps Stokes, leader of the delegation, called Father's attention at an opportune time to what Yale men would do with an empty pitcher. No one enjoyed this more than Father.

When an invitation was given me to join a fraternity I put the matter up to Father. He had never affiliated himself with any secret society and many of his friends were opposed to them. He left the matter entirely to me, taking the ground that he knew so little about college fraternities that he should not decide. I never felt he was in any measure displeased with me for accepting the invitation.

The ultra-pious were critical of him for allowing first my brother and then me to go to Yale when there were, particularly in the Middle West, so many colleges which placed more emphasis on orthodoxy. His reply to that was that my older brother had benefited in every way, spiritually and mentally, from his years at college, and if his younger son should profit as much he would be devoutly thankful. For that type of piety which wraps its offspring in cotton wool he had no use. He loved young people and knew they must be trusted.

One reason for his enjoyment of the Student Conferences was his genuine if quite untrained interest in games and sports. He built a tennis court on his lawn and he loved to watch games calling for action and skill. When he discovered Stagg at a Conference he was not satisfied till an exhibition game was arranged. His ardor was cooled when one day Charles Eastman, later to become the well-known Indian authority, was knocked unconscious by a ball pitched by Stagg. Races of all kinds he loved, particularly obstacle races. In his own very underprivileged youth he had loved running, one of the most primitive sports and one calling for little equipment. Even in his later years he could run twenty-five or thirty yards with great speed, despite his weight, and he used laughingly to challenge anyone who would carry enough ballast to equal his own considerable weight.

It was my father's lot, though with very little schooling in the formal sense, to make what he himself considered the greatest contribution of his day to the field of education. In like manner he made a marked impact on the church music of his day, though almost tone-deaf and unable to tell one tune from another. It is probably a caricature to say, as his family

used to, that he could not distinguish "Yankee Doodle" from "Rock of Ages" if the first was played slowly and the latter jazzed. Certainly he had something in common with the man who always knew "The Star-Spangled Banner" and the "Doxology" because the audience rose, but otherwise could not tell them apart. Driving about, he loved to sing "My

Soul Be on Thy Guard," but he always sang it on one note. Yet no one could have had a sounder appreciation for the effect of music in unifying an audience. He knew to a nicety when an audience had been prepared for the message, psychologically. If he never used this word, and I never remember hearing him, he had nevertheless a very wide working knowledge of what it represents.

It is a truism that the way to unify an audience is to get it to cry together or laugh together or sing together. Laughter is dangerous. Crying more so, and singing is the safest. He never moved his audience to laughter or tears for the sake of playing on it. He hated cheapness or sensationalism. But he did use singing and he wanted it hearty. It was because it was the preparation for the sowing of the seed. So he became a master of assemblies whether he was preaching or presiding. He knew that long passages of Scripture and long prayers kill the interest of an audience, and particularly the latter he abominated, saying that he suspected the lengthy prayer of making up in public what he lacked in his private devotions. He used to say that the first five minutes of a prayer he joined in thought with the petitioner. To the second five minutes he was passive, and then he prayed that his long-winded brother would stop.

The story of his awakening of Grenfell has been told many times. Grenfell, purely out of curiosity, had followed the crowd into one of the large meetings in London. A long-winded prayer was being offered, and Grenfell in impatience got up to leave when he was aware of a stocky, bearded figure rising and saying, "While our brother is finishing his prayer let us sing hymn number so and so." The startling informality of this arrested the young doctor and he waited to hear what such a man would say. The result was a revolution in his outlook on life which sent him as a medical missionary to that rocky shore and to a work which has been so remarkable that the two words, "Grenfell" and "Labrador," are forever associated.

Dr. Coffin told me this last summer of an experience one year at Northfield. A lean-faced fanatic was telling the students that unless they had agonized an entire night in prayer they did not know the meaning of the word. In a second my father, who was presiding, had his hand on the man's shoulder. "Hold on," he said, "I tried that once and woke up an awful stiff Moody." His viewpoint was nothing if not sane and his view of God prevented his subscribing to such conceptions. In like manner, once when an anti-evolutionist who had been invited to Northfield made a long and learned and somewhat boring attack on Evolution, the students in attendance were in revolt and a committee representing the Harvard, Yale, and Princeton delegations waited on Father to protest. It put him "on the spot." But the next morning he announced that the address of the day before had so much matter for thought that he knew it had not been digested and that instead of having the second address given on that warm morning he was going to have it published in the *Northfield Echoes* so that it could go around the world and everyone could read it. Meanwhile he was going to speak himself on "Gidjon." The embarrassing situation was saved. The learned gentleman purred with delight at the thought of his attack being read all around the world, the students chuckled and were satisfied, and a break was averted.

The stories of Grenfell and of the man who advocated "agonizing" illustrate his attitude toward prayer. It was quality, not quantity, that counted. Once in a crowded hotel I shared a room with him. His devotions before falling into bed were so exceedingly brief that I regretfully admit I was a trifle shocked. But the pace at which he lived enabled him to sleep at a second's notice and the attitude of his soul at all times was such that long prayers were unnecessary. We used laughingly to accuse him of catching naps on the platform when prayers were long. He would never admit or deny it. He had one valuable gift. He would drop off for five minutes at any time or in any place, and be soundly asleep. But no matter how soundly asleep he may have seemed, and

97

his deep breathing and sometimes snoring were evidence of this, he would be wide awake in an instant if a remark was made in a low tone with which he did not agree. I have never happened to see this in anyone else, but I witnessed it many times in his case and saw him come out of an apparently deep sleep to correct some misstatement or exaggeration.

His confession that he had tried futilely to pray all night is in line with other admissions. One of his associates made the boast that he took literally the injunction of the Sermon on the Mount to "give to him that asketh thee, and from him that would borrow of thee turn not thou away." Father in his own way made up his mind to try it. "The first day it cost me over a hundred dollars," he said, and he quit. And he used to say that his adviser, he found, emptied his pockets before he left his house and in reality evaded completely the injunction. This my father determined was a principle of the Kingdom and applicable only to those who accepted the King, and was not a rule for daily life for everyone.

VI

DUMONAL

THE care of the hens and the garden, the horses and cows, the fairly extensive lawns, and my mother's flower beds necessitated no small staff. Besides the servants in the house there was never less than one man, the "hired man" of New England, and in the summer two and sometimes more. Now and then it was a student who might vary his duties in the barn-yard with tutoring me — or be sent hurrying off to change his clothes in order to join us at the table when Father had some guest he desired to have this student meet. Once the work was done by an old self-respecting farmer with land of his own. And we all addressed him as Mr. Newton. I used to play tricks on him by nailing up certain of the sheds from the inside and crawling out through small apertures, too small for anyone else to crawl through. Then, of course, the proper technique would be to disappear. I am afraid that even the servants' toilet was not immune from my efforts. When hunger brought me back I would be — well, not exactly welcomed, but the object, let me say, of a good deal of interest. On occasions of this sort it was always my mother who spoke plainly and pointedly on the matter. I suspect that she knew my father would have been apt to appreciate the humor of the situation a little too keenly and mar the effect of the lecture by an ill-advised chuckle at the wrong point. For to the end of the chapter there was a good deal of the small boy about him.

There was more or less of the New England attitude of democracy about the place. We children were encouraged to wait on ourselves a good deal and we did not think or speak of those in the household as servants. They were "help." There was little of the hireling about them.

My father had one man about the place between whom and himself the attachment was deep. He was a grizzled old Frenchman, a veteran of the Franco–Prussian War as well as the war in Italy. We were never able to extract from him all of his military history, for he had learned his English from the Irish and he spoke a highly ungrammatical Irish brogue with a French accent. He appeared in Northfield when I was a small boy. For some reason or other he came to my father with a real or supposed grievance. Father's sympathies went out to him but he could not reinstate him without injustice to the school farmer, so to save face all around he hired him himself. The old man became the gardener on the home place, for we had to have a garden at home for the sake of fresh vegetables, in addition to Father's hobby. Soon his failing became evident. He was a sporadic drinker. He would go off on terrible sprees and be absent for days. After each escapade he returned repentant and was kept on. Soon the intervals between debauches became longer and longer. Finally he came to my mother with his salary and asked her to keep it for him. Nothing was said about his habit, but his request was obviously an admission that he could not look after it himself. This act on his part was the beginning of his final reformation. He ceased completely to go on any more sprees and his savings increased. And he began to go to church whenever he thought Father was speaking, and finally he became a more or less regular attendant at our church despite the fact that he was a Roman Catholic and kept up his contact with his own church. He understood nothing of what was said, but with a canine devotion he went to the house of God where my father went because my father went there. To him Father's word was law and gospel, and he was happiest when pottering about in the garden with my father, whose brisk walk he followed at a sort of dogtrot. He had one formula with which he always greeted the members of the family, "Papa, he good man, Mama, she good woman," and proceeding through the family he named us all, but with obviously lessening conviction.

That Father never made the least attempt

to persuade the old man to come to our church is very certain. The old man was quite incapable of any processes of cerebration but equally capable of doing whatever my father suggested to him. But there was a deeper reason. For my father the Catholic Church was a branch of the Church Universal, and for his attitude toward it he was often bitterly attacked. Many if not most of the Catholics in Northfield worked for the Seminary and so, he felt, were his associates, and when they built their church he gave them a gift and presented them with an organ. In some way this got out and that branch of the Church which is more Protestant than Christian had a field day. Though I do not recollect this distinctly, I do recall the continuance of the muttering of the rabid anti-papists for years afterward and his mild amusement at it. The sequel of his assistance to the Catholic Church is interesting. When we came to build a new and larger Congregational Church at Northfield the Catholics as their contribution drew all the stone for the foundation.

When the old man's savings had mounted to the neighborhood of a thousand dollars and upward, he suddenly disturbed the summer calm by announcing that he was going back to France. He had had little or no contact with his native land in the years we had known him — few if any letters. To our question if any of his family was living he could make no certain response. Everything was said to discourage him, but he would go. His money was drawn out of the bank for him by my mother and he set off. The weeks lengthened into months and over a year went by. He had sent no message and we all sadly concluded that in his native land away from his friends the old habit had gotten too much for him, and our household mourned to think we had seen the last of "Old Paul." The adjective, I might add, was used to avoid confusion. Sometimes he was "Paul the Frenchman." Then, after all hope was dead, he returned. Some grading was being done about the village church and Father had gone to see it, and I was with him. Up the long elm-shaded street came the station bus, and sitting in it, in a gray suit and brilliant red tie, was Old Paul. He and my father saw each other at the same time. Father ran and Paul scrambled over the wheels and they fell in each other's arms and with tears of joy embraced as though they had both been Frenchmen, and some of us watched through misted eyes, for we knew the happiness of each at seeing the other. Incredible as it may seem, the old man had brought all his savings back save the cost of the trip and what he had spent putting a new roof on a cottage where some of his relatives lived in France. And in a day or two he was installed in his old room on the place and working among his flowers and vegetables.

There he remained until his mind began to weaken. He had delusions of persecution. Father, who was home at the time, would not delegate to anyone else the sad duty of taking him to the Insane Asylum, but drove him there himself, and Paul went willingly if not gladly because my father deemed it best. The stay there was beneficial to such an extent that it was thought safe to release him, and he came back and worked again among his flowers. So it happened that he was still in our employ when Father died. The old man's grief was touching to see, and all the next summer, early in the morning or late in the evening, he could be seen trudging up the slope to Round Top where my father was buried — watering the grave, day after day, that the grass might be green. Round Top is sandy soil, but the old Frenchman's presence there was due more to his deep dumb sense of devotion than to the need of the roots of the grass for water, both equally instinctive.

Not long after this at his own request he went back to the Asylum, where he remained under the legal guardianship of my mother till her death. One of the last things she did was to transfer him to another hospital which she deemed better for him, and there he remained till a few years later he died and my brother and I buried him with the full rites of the Catholic Church in the little cemetery at Northfield.

MR. AND MRS. MOODY AND GRANDCHILDREN

The old man was never very articulate, and to understand the little he attempted to say was difficult to the point of impossibility. But he could sometimes make himself clear without words, and the complete self-abnegation and abandon with which he loved my father, his friend, touched and awakened full response in the latter. The relationship of employer and employee, of master and man, was lost in the finer one of friend and friend.

To say that my father was democratic is to misstate the case. He was democracy personified. Driving through the streets with him, I noticed that he always raised his hat to men as well as women. I asked him once why he saluted men this way when usually this was reserved for ladies. He replied that he always did. I think he felt he would not let anyone outdo him in courtesy, and he really respected his neighbors. Only from one man did I see this withheld. A neighbor who used sometimes to meet us would always bow ceremoniously. He got only the curtest nod. I asked why. He was a church member, but he had done a very shabby trick and defrauded a neighbor. My father had told him to refund the money or keep still in prayer meeting. He would do neither, so Father refused to acknowledge his acquaintance when they met. In this he was quite Pauline, for across the river there was a charming old reprobate who made no professions whatever. With him Father was on the best of terms and delighted always to run across him on the train or elsewhere, and he used to invite Father to preach in an open-air service in a grove he owned. Father would accept and the old scamp would busy himself providing chairs for old ladies and acting as an usher generally.

He once taught me a lesson in the dignity of labor. During the World's Fair in 1893 I was staying with him in the Bible Institute and he told me to carry his shoes to the shoe stand in the basement and black them for him. In the interests of decency it seemed to me that it would be more suitable to convey the shoes in a handbag — which unfortunately I did. On returning, also unfortunately, I met him. In a glance he sensed the situation and asked me if I had been ashamed to carry his shoes through the lobby. I replied, "Not ashamed, exactly, but it seemed a little more proper not to advertise what one was doing." He was n't smiling when he told me of an English peer who had been staying with him who always carried his shoes in his hand to black them. What an English peer could do he seemed to imagine I could. And when he got through, I could. Snobbery of any sort was forever utterly intolerable to him. If a thing needed to be done it was a distinction to be able to do it. After all, as Shorthouse says, "constant attendance at the Court of the King of Kings renders one more than a little indifferent to human distinctions."

VII

AT WORK

ALTHOUGH I heard him the last time he preached at the Schools at Northfield, I cannot recall the first time I ever heard him. It must have been when I was very young. Nor did I ever, because of my tender years at first and later because of the interference of education, attend regularly throughout any of his preaching missions either in this country or abroad. But often I was with him for days or weeks as he preached in New York or Chicago or Boston and would go then to many meetings. During the greater part of the time he spoke regularly twice a day, but oftener the two preaching services would be followed by meetings for inquirers, those who had just made a profession of faith, so that he was frequently speaking four times a day six days a week and that for weeks on end. Some of his sermons I heard many, many times, like the one on "Sowing and Reaping," and the character sermons on David and Gideon. Practically all of these sermons are in print.

The students of homiletics will read these sermons to-day with a sense of wonder that they moved men to the extent they did. This is inevitable, as some sermons should be heard, not read, precisely as others should be read and not heard. The best of ghost writers could not preserve in the written sermon all the force it had when delivered. The informality is missing. With the elimination of the homely aphorism, the colloquialism, grammatical slips, and rapid elisions, much was bound to go. The newspapers of the day, which often reported him verbatim, much to his embarrassment, give the clearest impression. When he knew he was being taken down verbatim he worked in as much direct quotation from the Bible as he could. But he was nervous on such occasions, though audiences did not suspect it, for he was so keenly aware of his own early lack of education.

He often said that he could never have taken a church with the necessity of writing fresh sermons every week. I think he did himself an injustice in this respect, for, while under the

pressure of the tremendous amount of work he did he had to fall back on addresses he had given before, he did prepare new sermons and revise old ones in the leisure he had in the early mornings at Northfield. I say prepare, for he did not write. His mind worked much too fast for his hand. He prepared outlines, writing them in his large hand on the four sides of ordinary correspondence paper. These he kept in blue linen envelopes on the outside of which were written the dates and places where they were used. Into these envelopes he would thrust anything which related to the subject until they were often very full. His verbal memory was at once good and bad. He did not quote poetry unless it was the familiar line of a hymn. I never remember seeing or hearing him read any quotations. He talked much too rapidly to allow anything of this sort to break the continuity.

Indeed, he talked so fast that, like his contemporary Phillips Brooks, he was the despair of reporters. And he made the task no easier by his constant colloquialisms and elisions. He had what has been called "the gamy flavor of a bookless man." The pithy sayings of the countryside he had heard as a barefooted boy he used to his dying day, and picked up others — "quick'n chain lightnin'," "hir'n Haman," "drier'n Gidjon's fleece." This last one was

often on his lips in describing long-winded or
sententious sermons which seemed to his quick
mind so dull. Sir Alexander Simpson always
declared that he pronounced Jerusalem in two
syllables. He just could n't be bothered about
unimportant details, and when he had written
enough letters of a word to signify its import,
he let the rest go. His letters were not invariably easy to read. I never heard him say "Daniel" or "Samuel." Few Yankees do. It was
"Dan'l" and "Sam'l" and "Gidjon." What
were superfluous syllables between friends,
anyhow?

In his study, which was upstairs, he had relatively few books — Spurgeon's sermons and
Bibles, but little else. In the library, which was
more living room than library, the walls were
lined with tightly packed shelves. Looking
over many of these, I find marks which could
have been no other than his, and in his earlier
days he must have read these, for he generally
knew the gist of them. But in the period of
which I write and in which alone I remember
him he did not read much. He spent his time

preparing for the next preaching mission, going over his notes and refreshing them. There was little time for intensive work when a campaign was once on.

During a good part of the summer he would be presiding morning and evening at meetings, earlier in the Conferences in Stone Hall and later in the Auditorium. In the early afternoon he usually took a nap, and it was a regular one, deliberately going to bed in his upstairs study where he had a massive folding bed. And a good part of the time when not otherwise occupied he would be signing, literally by the thousand, the typed begging letters he was sending out for money for the increasing needs of his expanding Schools. For they were growing to such an extent that the proceeds from the sale of the hymnbooks was not adequate to supplement the modest charges. He was very fastidious about these letters. He would not have them signed by a rubber stamp and he did not like to have them blotted. He wanted the ink to dry, and the room, floor and furniture, would be covered by these myriad letters.

These letters to be signed followed him, too, on his preaching missions, and he carried this load at all times. He might have put on a drive for an endowment, but he did not like the idea of endowments, feeling that they usually had a deadening effect upon institutions. He liked living endowments, the support of a large army of people who gave yearly small gifts and whose interest was maintained in this way and often increased. He felt there was more value in having a thousand people give ten dollars each than in a gift of a thousand dollars from one individual. He was not unaware that it cost more and he did not discourage larger gifts, but he felt the spread of interest and support was worth the added cost. His attitude toward money was peculiar. As a young man entering business he had set his heart on a certain sum. But when the Gospel had its way with him, and after a struggle which he describes as the severest he ever underwent, he turned his back on money-making. He seemed almost afraid of money, and any that came to him he got rid of as quickly as possible, keeping only enough for the demands of our simple if hospitable home. He repeatedly said quite cheerfully that he did not want to leave his children anything but work and he wanted to leave them plenty of that. I do not think in the decision to give up business it was possible possession of money that counted as much as the struggle or the game. It was never the quarry that interested him in business, it was the quest. Had the grace of God not found him he would have been a great gambler in legitimate ways. Indeed he always was in another sense. He loved contests and games of skill or chance, though he would not play cards, having the common prejudice of his day against them. He did play "Authors" delightedly as a relaxation. And he found plenty of opportunities to take a chance in the interests of the Kingdom of God. His going to England in 1873 with a wife and two children and Mr. and Mrs. Sankey dependent upon him, with no human backing, is an instance of this. His founding of the three Schools is another. But he never overlooked any preparation he could make to ensure success.

On the occasions when I was with him on preaching missions he was busy all the time. He almost invariably stayed at hotels latterly, though formerly in friends' houses. He preferred the greater and necessary freedom and he accepted few invitations to private houses. In his choice of hotels he often disregarded the arrangements of committees, feeling the accommodations were too pretentious, and small temperance hotels, particularly abroad, appealed to him most. There was always a coming and going of visitors and friends, and constant issuing of orders, for every detail was, as far as possible, planned carefully. He would depart in an instant from a prearranged plan if need presented itself. He was never stereotyped and his developed sense of the psychology of an audience told him infallibly when to sing and when to preach and what to do if interest was waning or if some benevolent but stupid associate was unconsciously lowering

the temperature necessary for the acceptance
of the message. What he would do was unpredictable. I once sat on the bench with a friend
who is a judge. In the midst of a trial he sud-

denly declared a recess. In his chambers I
asked him why. "Juror number seven was
sleepy and the evidence at this point is crucial,"
he replied. Father would have understood that

perfectly. No detail was too small. Drafts, bad lighting, overofficious ushers, half-hearted singing — all these things were under his watchful eye and nothing could be allowed which interfered with his object. Offerers of long prayer, announcers of long or unnecessary notices, bores and cranks, were brushed aside as painlessly as possible, but effectually.

His sermons were delivered over and over as I have said, but never at the same mission unless in different parts of the city or in response to requests. And many of these I heard repeatedly. Yet they always had a sufficiently varied handling so that I listened as interestedly the tenth time as the first. And I have found myself as held and riveted as anyone who had never heard him before. He would say sometimes not to go for he was preaching a sermon I had heard. But I never remember missing an opportunity to hear him speak. As I grew older and more critical generally I listened as intently as ever. Only once do I remember listening with any apprehension and that was when he preached overtime in my freshman year, to

No Detail Was Too Small for Him

which circumstance I have referred. But I alone seemed worried.

How he stood the strain of these meetings I do not know. His giant physique did in the end, of course, suffer. He said to me a month before he died that he expected to reach the normal span of three score and ten. He slept soundly and ate well and always took one day in seven for complete rest, if it could be called that. He never seemed to worry and he appeared to dismiss what was done when it was over. My mother, as I have said, spared and shielded him to the limit of her ability. Exercise as such when away from home he never took. In fact, as he grew stouter he took little anyway, and he avoided unnecessary physical exertion, for he knew the strain placed upon his heart. His voice was equal to any occasion in that day before amplifiers and it was not unusual to talk to audiences of ten or even fifteen thousand, and sometimes outdoors.

VIII

IRA D. SANKEY

IT may be owing to a defective sense of humor, but I never did like the verse of a music-hall song that had a vogue when I was small, to the effect that while, quite inelegantly, the "youngest son was the son of a gun,"

> The eldest son was a nice young man
> Got up on the Moody and Sankey plan.

It is possibly the reference to the younger son, notoriously touchy since the days of the prodigal and probably long before that. It is, of course, possible that my dislike was based on an early and instinctive recoil from the adjective "nice," an always rather prickly one. Perhaps it is because I heard that particular verse much, much too often, for I grieve to say it was sometimes sung in my honor. There are times when music does not soothe. But in all probability my dislike of the verse was and still is founded on my humble but quite biased childish feeling that it was *lèse-majesté* to mention any other name in connection with my father's and that he was not only the main tent but the whole show, down to the dog under the wagon. Such is childish prejudice, and sometimes these prejudices linger on and we do not recognize them.

In my defense, however, it may be said that by the time I was old enough to go to meetings Mr. Sankey was past his prime and his singing was no longer the feature it had been, and he was accompanying my father less and less. This was not so much because his voice was aging as because he was no longer able to stand the kind of strain Father himself underwent and put his singers under. It was not at all unusual for Father to wear out two or three or even four singers in the course of a winter's meetings. Father was tough and you had to be tough to keep up with him, and since this Mr. Sankey no longer was, they were together gradually less and less in the winter. It is said, though I cannot give chapter and verse for the statement, that at one series of meetings Father spoke two hundred and eighty-five times to audiences averaging over seven thousand. Mr. Sankey's physique was not up to this, and small wonder.

I have been told many, many times by those who remembered him in his prime that his voice was the most moving and compelling they ever heard. I can testify to its volume and its tones. Mr. Sankey, I suppose, was what is called to-day a "natural." He had very little training and was not a professional singer. As a matter of fact he was in the Internal Revenue Department when he and my father met, and my father persuaded him to give up his position, which paid him well for those days, and to join up with him. All this was, of course, long before I was born and I write only of hearsay. When Mr. Sankey went with my father on the first mission in 1873 it was on a guarantee from my father, and he was even a trifle dubious about the wisdom of printing the hymnbooks.

Had Mr. Sankey been better trained he might possibly have lasted longer as a singer and might have been able to protect his marvelous voice better. But when it is recalled where and how and how often he used his voice, there is small wonder that in the eighties it was largely a thing of the past. It is very certain that he made full use of it, and he probably sang often when he should have saved himself. But he was less and less with my father in the days I remember and I have little or no recollection of him apart from Northfield. There I remember him very distinctly, for he bought a house there which he made his summer home. He lived in Brooklyn in the winter. His house in Northfield was in the centre of the old town, perhaps a mile from our house. He was always very kind to me and I remember him as a very jovial man, far more conventional in dress than my father and rather given to frock coats and silk hats, thus presenting a good deal of a contrast to my father's far more informal appearance. He even wore the old-fashioned gray topper which we associate with the English aristocracy at garden parties, Epsom, and Lord's. He had no such passion for the country life and amateur farming as my father had and apart from my father had no close associations with Northfield — no deep roots there or boyhood memories. He had been born and brought up in Pennsylvania. He had three sons, the oldest of whom died before I remember. The two younger sons were just enough beyond me in years to prevent any intimacy, but Mrs. Sankey I remember distinctly as one of the loveliest and most gracious women I ever knew. Like my own mother, she was very retiring and disinclined to appear in public.

It was inevitable that while the mutual respect and affection remained constant, the association between Father and Mr. Sankey lessened. Mr. Sankey's contribution to the — shall we say — partnership was bound by its very nature to diminish as the years took toll of his really golden voice, while all the time my father was growing. Of the two my father was by temperament better equipped to meet the dangers always attendant on growing fame, for the one thing which always impressed those who came into closest and most intimate contact with him was his essential humility and modesty, however he may have impressed others who did not know him.

For a lesser man than Mr. Sankey this growing difference of stature would have been too hard to bear, and it may not have been easy for him when he realized the day had come when people who showed no feverish anxiety to hear him sing were glad to hear my father speak. For it must have dawned on him that he no longer pulled such a strong oar in the boat as once he had pulled and his contribution to the joint endeavor was decreasing while that of his friend was increasing. I never knew of his showing any signs of jealousy, but he tried all the harder, I think, and he became a little heavy and pompous, and mannerisms grew upon him at which some of the thoughtless used to laugh, and this never failed to hurt my father. In Mr. Sankey's eagerness to contribute his share he often talked about the solo he was to sing and sometimes talked a little too long, till one was reminded of Rossetti's elaborate preparation of a frame for a picture before he painted it, sometimes even writing a sonnet about it till Whistler with his caustic wit suggested that he frame the sonnet.

But if, as the years went by, they worked together less often, there was never any lessening of affection and certainly never such a break as occurred between two of their contemporaries whose names are equally linked, Gilbert and Sullivan. No one, I am sure, outside the immediate family was more saddened by my father's death. He was three years younger and he outlived my father by nearly nine years, becoming in the end entirely blind. He lived in and for the hymns he had made so popular, bringing out new editions of them and writing about them. It is impossible to estimate the value of the contribution he made to the success of the earlier missions and I am the last one to attempt such an estimate.

The two were very congenial and alike in many respects, especially in their love of fun, though I hope I am doing no injustice in saying that Mr. Sankey never seemed to relish jokes upon himself to quite the extent my father did, a fact which rather stimulated that impish sense which was seldom far from the surface in my father.

Mr. Sankey must have been an extremely handsome man in his youth, for he was still a striking figure when I knew him, portly, well-dressed, a little on the old-fashioned side, with gray sideburns, a style which the princely Drummond always adopted and which my father himself followed in his earlier days. It may have been these sideburns which inspired my father to recommend them to me — the one piece of advice he ever gave me in which I saw no sense. My face was too long and narrow, Father declared, a premise with which I could not of course disagree, but with the deduction that it would be improved by side whiskers I did, violently. He reverted to it many times, urging it strongly. But I was adamant. The thought of returning to college with side whiskers was as repulsive as the thought of taking back a goatee. They were not being worn at Yale even in those days, and for that matter they had even gone out of fashion in England. Gillette and Burma Shave had not at that time completed their reform of the facial landscape of the Victorian Era, but a better day was coming. I agreed heartily with a friend who declared that while undoubtedly Providence sent us some of our troubles, side whiskers were strictly a man's own fault. But Father would always say, "Think of the time you waste in shaving!"

IX

TRAVEL

IT was my good fortune to be with my father on the only occasion when he traveled at leisure, for though he traveled much it was always as a means to an end with an object in view, not as an end in itself. He went to Great Britain in all some seven times and on several of these trips he was on the Continent. He would, I believe, have gone abroad oftener, he had so many friends in Great Britain and was exceedingly fond of it, but he was the worst sailor I have ever encountered and began to feel ill on going up the gangplank. The least motion of the boat upset him dreadfully. How far this was psychological I do not know. He was not imaginative in respect to himself. As he grew stouter the doctors felt and declared that he was actually in danger, so great was his distress. The one time when he was able to rise above this disability was when he returned from Great Britain in 1892 on the German liner the *Spree*. A few days out from Queenstown she broke her propeller, flooded the two rear compartments, and was unable to make any headway. My brother was alone with him. On the realization of danger my father rose from his berth and was active for the balance of the trip. It was some years before Marconi had completed his experiments with the wireless and we on shore were in ignorance of the situation, though as the boat was long overdue our anxiety was acute. It was not until the disabled liner had been picked up and towed back to Queenstown that we received the cablegram which set us at rest.

The occasion to which I have referred was his visit to Palestine. He had long talked about it, but it was little more than a dream at the back of his mind. In the spring of 1892, however, at the conclusion of his meetings and after the rest of the family had spent the winter on the Continent or in Egypt, Mr. and Mrs. Peter McKinnon of Scotland invited my father and mother to be their guests in a trip to the Holy Land, and I was taken with them. The party was joined at Paris by an American friend and his son, a boy of my own age. Naturally a good deal of my time was spent with this very congenial young friend.

On the trip from Alexandria to Joppa on an indescribable Egyptian boat, Father met several people who interested him greatly. One was a young Russian, a priest of the Greek Church by the name of Tolstoi and a relative of the great novelist. He had a face of great beauty and spirituality and, bearded, resembled pictures of Christ. Father was strongly drawn to him. He spoke English, though not fluently, and he had come to Palestine to see if a visit to the shrines there could resolve some of the doubts and distresses which had arisen in his mind. He looked very troubled and Father had several talks with him and was deeply impressed by him. We ran into him several times in Jerusalem and found that from the standpoint of the object of his journey his visit had been far from successful. His unhappiness and unrest were increasing. Later we learned that he had sought anchorage in the Church of Rome.

There was also on board an English Bishop, a gracious and cultivated man whose wife was the daughter of a very prominent Duke. Though Scotch, her ladyship was more Anglican than her husband, but equally gracious and cultivated. Her great preoccupation on the trip was to persuade my father that he ought to take orders, and she did her best to persuade him that he should not speak in public again until he had been consecrated by the laying on of hands by authorities of the Church of England. She was very sincere and charming if unconvincing to my father, who thoroughly enjoyed talking with her and her husband. Her insistence on his receiving the proper qualifications for preaching the Gospel got under the skin of the other members of the party, but I remember only my father's good-natured amusement at it. They parted the best of friends, she still insisting on the necessity of conformity to her views.

On that same wretched boat we had a service on Good Friday. It fell on April 15 that year. We landed that afternoon at Joppa and

were driven to Jerusalem. The railroad at that time was in process of construction and we could see the tracks being laid. We arrived in Jerusalem at three in the morning, as all of the party wished to spend Easter Sunday there.

On this Easter Sunday Father preached at the request of the missionaries on the summit of what is supposed by some to have been Calvary. I think he felt keenly the uncertainty which attaches to so many of the sites in the city. He unconsciously gave offense to devout Mohammedans, for inadvertently he had preached in the centre of a Moslem burying ground. The following Sunday he spoke from the side of the hill where there could be no question. His theme was "As the mountains are round about Jerusalem," and he spoke of the events in the past connected with the very hills we could see as he talked.

One experience is more vivid to me than to other members of the party. We were being shown through the Mosque of Omar and in accordance with custom had either to remove our shoes or to put over them slippers furnished by the authorities to prevent non-Moslem feet from treading on holy ground. One of mine came off, unnoticed by anyone at first, and I profaned some yards of the sacred carpet before it was discovered. Then a terrible hubbub arose and Arab eloquence was poured out in every direction while I stood on one foot, not a little scared, as were my parents. The slipper was finally retrieved, the ears of the erring attendant who had carelessly fastened it duly boxed, and we went on amid the muttering of the scandalized Moslems. But we were all relieved to get out.

Travel in Palestine at that time was difficult. The roads were bad and some were practically impossible for carriages, so what Father saw outside Jerusalem was only those places to which he could be driven and these were relatively few. He did see Bethlehem and Hebron, but not the Jordan. The Jordan and Jericho were visited by those of the party who could ride donkeys or horses, but this was out of the question for Father.

While he was loath to admit it I think on the whole the trip was a disappointment to him. The sight of Moslem guards at the Holy Sepulchre and at the Church of the Nativity at Bethlehem to keep the Christians from fighting wounded him deeply. He did so hate differences among Christians. And the uncertainty relating to other places was unsatisfactory. He had at his disposal the best-informed students on the archæology of Jerusalem. The Honorable Selah Merrill, for many years American Consul at Jerusalem, was often his guide and he was long a student of the sacred city and was well informed. And Cook's representative in Palestine was at our disposal. But all students disagreed about so many sites that it was disturbing.

Other things stand out clearly. One is a drive through the streets of Cairo alone with Father. According to his custom he was plying our native driver, who spoke what passed for English, with questions about conditions in Egypt. The driver was regaling him with some quite imaginary details. It happened that I had read something of the recent history of Egypt and objected strongly, with boyish omniscience, to the misinformation being so freely furnished, and I protested. I received a dig in the ribs from his elbow which almost dislodged me and an admonition to be quiet. "I want to know what *he* thinks," said my father. It was his custom to interrogate anyone with whom he chanced to be thrown in contact. He could and did avail himself of the correct information at the proper time, but it was his invariable habit to pump information from everyone in whatever walk of life. People, he knew, love to impart information. It ministers to their sense of importance, and he liked to know what the man in the street actually thought, whether it was right or wrong.

I drove alone with him again in Rome along the Appian Way. Learning that some distance out the original pavement could in places be seen, we drove until we reached it. Then he insisted on alighting, desiring to walk over the stones which might have been pressed by the feet of Saint Paul. There was too much uncertainty relating to many of the other places, both in Rome and in Palestine. But over that pavement of the Appian Way he was positively as excited as an antiquarian.

It is perhaps understandable that to a boy of my age the bright spot of the whole trip was a morning spent on an Italian lake, on our way back to Paris. There my father and I chartered a small boat rowed by an Italian who furnished the tackle. I remember much good-natured banter before we set out. A childish diary kept at that time records that "Mrs. McKinnon said she would give us half a crown for every one we caught and Mama said 'five dollars.'" It was n't exactly sport, for we trolled with lines supplied with about twenty hooks each and our "bag" was "126 fish not *very* small" (the diary again). They were served to us for breakfast announced on the menu as "fish *à la* Moody." My father's enjoyment of the sport I am sure exceeded mine. The entry for the following day in this little diary may account for the desire my father showed that I might have some fun, for the next day being Sunday the entry is as follows: "In the morning we had a service or Bible reading, we had one in the afternoon and one in the evening. 'To [*sic*] much of a thing is good for nothing.' I was very tired of it and those Scotch would propose a Bible reading every chance they got." I am afraid I did not show due regard for the tastes of Father's friends, our generous hosts. In retrospect I am sure it was my own unprompted Puritan conscience which kept me in attendance, for it is not my recollection of my father's way of treating a thirteen-year-old boy. I probably argued with myself that it would show disrespect to be absent. I am very sure from other remembrances that it would have been characteristic of him to have spared me, for I can distinctly recall his efforts to protect other children from overdoses of church services when too enthusiastic parents miscalculated the powers of absorption of their offspring.

A rereading of that old and battered record, in very childish hand and even more childish wording, shows that wherever he went, in Palestine, in Egypt or Italy, he was an assiduous sight-seer. Our party was so large, however, and with usually such differing interests that we were seldom all together. I do not recall "doing" the sights of Naples or Florence with him, though I do recall the demands upon him for preaching and for Bible readings wherever the English-speaking people knew of his presence.

Seven years later, the last summer he was alive, he surprised me by saying to someone, in my presence, that when I had graduated from college I would want to go around the world and he was going with me. He was always extremely anxious to see Australia and he had received many invitations to go there. And he would have liked to see the Orient and visit the missions there, many of them by this time manned by men and women who had been at the Schools at Northfield. I think he would have gone before had he not been such a poor sailor. As he died in my junior year at college, this dream was not realized.

I cannot think of a more ideal companion for a trip around the world. Everywhere he went people knew him and were anxious to do all they could for him. He was such a good sport in regard to hardships, laughing at them. He never went out of his way to encounter them and he preferred comfort to discomfort.

There was no hair-shirt complex in his make-up. And in addition he was always so keenly interested in everything he saw and avid for information. His careful reading of the papers made him familiar with most modern history. And he liked, as I have said, to glean information from anyone who could tell him anything, — sailors, railroad men, stewards, coachmen, — his real democratic instincts being felt by all he met. He "got next," to use the vernacular, to nearly everybody he met, that he wanted to. The snob, the bore, the crank, he sidestepped with dexterity and alacrity.

X

THE SCHOOLS

THE Northfield Seminary having been born the same year I was, I have no actual recollection of its beginning. But I have heard the story so many times and played such long hours on rainy days in the small rooms called Penny Alley, where the first girls were housed, that I feel as if I had been a witness of its start. My father was driving with the brother who, I think, was closest to him along one of his favorite back roads. There, before a very simple, probably unpainted cottage, he saw a farmer, who was crippled, plaiting straw hats with his three daughters. I do not think he stopped, but he and his brother discussed what there could be in life for these girls and how few advantages they could have. Northfield Seminary was born on that drive. Here was an outlet for the money the sale of his hymnbooks was bringing in. When he had realized that the sale of the books was great and would, if he was not careful, make him wealthy, he and Mr. Sankey had asked three conspicuous philanthropists to distribute this money for them, and it had been allotted to worthy causes.

These three men were William E. Dodge of New York, George Stuart of Philadelphia and John V. Farwell of Chicago. Mr. Edmund Coffin, father of Dr. Henry Sloane Coffin, served as legal counsel for this group and I have heard him describe his despair at getting my father to put his mind on the matters which came before the committee. Father, he said, did not seem to care what happened to the money provided he was n't bothered with it. It is a rather typical scene, I imagine: the financiers brought up with a wholesome respect for money and their incorrigible young friend who could n't be bothered about it, gladly signing without careful reading any document the import of which was to prevent his personally benefiting by money legally his.

There was always but a short jump from the idea to the operation with my father. He did not wait for anything, but since he was to be away that winter his house would do to begin in, and it did. The first girls slept in the house and their lessons were held there. But at once he began constructing other buildings. I can remember vaguely, not the earliest ones, but some very early ones. As the School grew and absorbed more land our home was practically surrounded by the campus. As a small boy I sometimes was taken by my father to the chapel exercises when he conducted them. It was typical of his informality. The reunions of the School I attend with clenched teeth to this day, so many dear old ladies recall having held me in their laps and insist on recounting incidents utterly forgotten by me — and some probably purely imaginary.

Father had been a warm friend of Henry Fowle Durant, the founder of Wellesley College, and was long a trustee of Wellesley, and there in part he got his inspiration for the Northfield Seminary. A study of any history of education in New England makes it clear how few high schools there were in those days. Private schools were few in number and high in price. He saw the need and with characteristic impetuosity started to meet it. One of his favorite mottoes was, as I have said, "Don't wait for something to turn up. Go and turn up something."

The most characteristic thing I ever saw him do was in our village church on one of those rare Sundays when he worshiped there. It was a Communion Sunday and the elderly deacons were passing the sacraments with characteristic benevolent inefficiency. His quick eye detected some pews that were overlooked. In a second he had risen, gone to the table, taken bread and wine, passed it, replaced the cup and the plate, and taken his seat again. It never occurred to him that, first, he was not a deacon or, second, that he had on rubber boots, as he did. Something needed to be done. He did it. He loved to say that any fool could eat soup with a spoon. It required brains to do it with a one-tined fork.

So with the Seminary. Unqualified to select teachers, he selected a principal to do it for him. After several years of the trial-and-error method he found a young woman, little more than a girl, who had recently graduated from Wellesley. He overrode her natural hesitancy and she accepted the headship of the School. From that day till the day of his death she was, next I think to my mother, his most trusted associate. His respect for her judgment knew no bounds. When they differed in policy he gave in to her. And she, without compromising her own educational standards, seconded his aims and hopes to an unusual degree.

It has been said that my father was a shrewd judge of character. I do not think he was. He always saw in people more than was there and was frequently disappointed. When aware of a mistake he usually corrected it, but not always, for in his large patience and charity he carried some of his associates who were sore trials to him. To him! If he felt they actually hindered or retarded the Kingdom of God, he parted company with them. But Evelyn Hall,

148

the young and efficient principal of the Seminary, was one in whom he felt increasingly he had made no mistake.

The three things which distinguished the Seminary were: first, the place of the Bible as an integral part of the curriculum; second, the participation of the students in the domestic work of the School, with two results — lessons in the dignity of labor and true democracy, and in the economy of operation; third, the low charge; for during his lifetime but one hundred dollars was asked for board, lodging, and tuition. The per capita cost was always about twice this. He looked upon it as his privilege to raise the other hundred by tireless and constant solicitation of small gifts.

Anyone connected with education will realize that these are sound principles, particularly the inclusion of manual work. That he, so lacking in formal education, built so wisely is owing to his great sanity and powers of observation.

Two years after the Seminary opened he started with this same ridiculously humble beginning the school for boys, now Mount Hermon, five miles from Northfield and on the west bank of the Connecticut River. In those motorless days it was practically an hour's distance. It was founded along the same lines save that here the work of the farm as well as within the buildings was done by the students. I speak from knowledge. I washed dishes or served as a waiter to a herd of cows while I lived there as a boarder.

Mount Hermon, more remote and younger, never became, it seemed to me, quite as close to his heart as the first-born of his projects. He was surrounded by his girls. His boys were five miles away, and added to this Miss Hall was longer in his service than anyone else and certainly more trusted.

In 1889 he founded the last of his Schools, the Bible Institute in Chicago, which, like the other Schools, has flourished and grown and rendered a great service. It was my privilege to be there with him only once when it was very young, the year of the World's Fair, so I do not have the recollection of him in connection with it. This is neither a biography nor an appraisal, but only my recollections of him. I do know how very dear it was to him and what a vast amount of effort and thought went into it. But it was not in Northfield, which he loved, but in Chicago. Of all cities he was fondest of Chicago, I believe. There he really began his service for the King. There he met and wooed his wife. But at heart he remained a country boy and the hills he had looked upon as a barefooted boy had done their work upon him, and Northfield was home!

In the same small unpretentious way the Conferences started — again before my recollections begin. I do remember very vaguely the Student Conference in 1886 when the Student Volunteer Movement was launched, and that memorable summer when Henry Drummond delivered that address on I Corinthians XIII, to be known for a generation as "The Greatest Thing in the World." When I was old enough to notice they had grown to considerable size. The General Conference for Christian Workers was first in point of time. Then the Students' Conference, and finally so many young women came to the Students' Conference, interfering in the sight of some of the leaders with the deeper aims of the Conference, that the Young Women's Conference was started. The buildings of the School at Northfield were used to house the attendants at these Conferences and in 1894 the Auditorium was built. Father was told it could never be filled. He laughed. It was crowded repeatedly the first year of its erection.

That which pleased my father most in both Schools was the opportunity he had of coming into close relationship with the students. Many of them, both boys and girls, had come there as a result of personal contact with him during his missions and he followed their careers in school with deep and intelligent interest. From one of the girls, now a woman, I received only recently a long letter telling of her early experiences and of her impressions. She happens to be one who has done a very remarkable piece of service since her graduation. But let her tell her own story.

In 1893, when the great Moody and Sankey meetings were being held in ——, my sister suggested that we have a talk with Mr. Moody about our future. Although we were worried because everything looked exceedingly dark to us, nevertheless, we felt that somehow or other we would be Providentially cared for.

Several years previous to the Evangelist's coming to the city, my father had failed, mother had passed away, and the home and furnishings were to be sold at auction within a few weeks.

While we were conversing with Mr. Moody, the thought of losing our beloved home filled me with deep grief and I broke down weeping. He turned to me asking, "How would you like to go to my school?" Between sobs I replied, "I did n't know you had one, and anyhow I am too old." This remark amused him very much, and he added, "Why, my dear child, even schoolteachers go there to polish up in their studies." His great, warm, tender heart must have been keenly touched, for as we were leaving the meeting, although there were many people waiting to talk with him, nevertheless he followed me to the door, urging me to come to see him the next morning at nine o'clock at the hotel, which I did; it was then that he told me of the many girls who attended the Seminary and of his desire to have me enter.

My father and I had always been close companions and as I was talking over with him Mr. Moody's kind offer he said, "Because of losing everything else, I cannot part with you also." On telling this to Mr. Moody he made no comment, but quietly answered, "Tell your father to come down in the morning to see me at this same hour," thus depicting the truth which I have often heard said of him that "he leaves no stone unturned in order to accomplish what he feels led to do." After Father's interview with Mr. Moody he said, "Daughter, I think you had better take advantage of this great opportunity; Mr. Moody wishes to see you again to-morrow morning." The next day, upon entering the room, Mr. Moody's first greeting was, "Now that your father has consented, everything is settled and I have sent a telegram to Miss Hall, the principal, telling her that I have found a new 'daughter-in-Christ.'" At this moment Mr. Sankey appeared in the doorway, and Mr. Moody beckoned to him saying, "Come in, Sankey; I want you to tell this young woman about Northfield, for I wish her to go there." Then Mr. Sankey told of the beauties of the campus, of the many buildings and of the Connecticut River which formed the letter S just where it borders the school grounds. Laughingly he said, "Providence must have meant that the Seminary should be placed right there because of this peculiar formation of the river." Mr. Moody then continued, saying, "I am sending you on my personal scholarship, but do not let this be a millstone around your neck, for if you can never, in the future, return the tuition fee it will be all right. I have mapped out two routes to Northfield from which you may choose; deep snows are there now, but my man will meet you at the station and take you to your destination."

Mr. Moody always quietly watched with keen interest the boys and girls whom he personally sent to the Schools. One evening he took me for a short drive, for he wanted to talk with me about an unexpected incident that had come into my life which was sorely troubling me at the time. While driving along he said that he had told his wife he could not sleep that night until he had explained more fully why this particular grief (which he knew all about) had come to me and what adjustment could be made. I marvel now at the tenderness and kindness of this great man, who had so many intricate problems to solve; to think that he would take time to go over this matter which was bothering little me! Had I realized, at the time, how wonderful and unusual this rare man was, I would have been awe-struck over the knowledge of his unusual abilities in many ways, as well as his strong spiritual power, and would have been grateful beyond words to think that he should have taken any cognizance of me. On the way back from our drive, he said that I had fitted in with the school life just as he had predicted two years ago, and that if after finishing, I wished to go on to college he would make it possible for me to do so! He then stopped the horse, bared his head and dedicated me to God and humanity; from that time on I felt every moment of my life should be given in service to others.

During the summer, as well as in winter, the Seminary took the place of home to me, and together with many other students, my time was spent on the campus working in connection with the great conferences. The last four summers while there, the privilege of having charge of Betsy Moody cottage, being matron as well as hostess, was given me. This dormitory, named for Mr. Moody's mother, housed the conference speakers, such as Margaret Sangster, John R. Mott, Robert E. Speer, Dr. Weston of the Crozier Theological Seminary, Mr. and Mrs. Sankey, as well as **Mr. Charles R. Otis, of the Otis Elevator Com-**

pany, and his wife. It was a rare opportunity for me, not only in a business way, but because coming in contact with these unusual people gave me a different outlook on life, which I afterwards strongly felt was a preparation for my present life's work.

One morning of the first summer when this responsibility was mine, Mr. Moody was driving by the cottage and seeing me on the steps asked, "What are you doing there?" Being so full of happiness over my new position, I spontaneously replied, "Oh, Mr. Moody, I have entire charge of this cottage!" Standing in the buggy, he took off his hat, and as he waved it said, "Three cheers! Three cheers!" This so startled his horse, Nelly, that she gave a leap which sent him hastily to his seat; nevertheless, not to be daunted he leaned out the side of the buggy as he sped down the road calling out, "You see, even old Nelly rejoices with me." Bless his heart! Thus his personal interest ran throughout the different phases of our life's work at the Seminary, and we all realized that we had in him not only a spiritual advisor, but one with interest akin to that of an earthly father for his children.

I cite this merely as typical. It could be duplicated a hundred times. The students at

Mount Hermon and Northfield were his sons and daughters, and into their joys and sorrows, their victories and defeats, he entered wholeheartedly and sympathetically. Even when the numbers grew to such an extent that he could not know them all, there were always enough who did know him to make his influence felt. He took a boyish delight in, once or twice a year on a day of unusual beauty, calling for "mountain day" and suspending all studies. Then he would go with the boys or the girls up into the mountains, a huge picnic being planned and corn or watermelons or some other appropriate thing being taken in quantities.

He always enjoyed, on the arrival or departure of the students, taking a pair of horses and a carriage and crowding in as many as he could and driving them to or from the station. He liked to do this when the Student Conferences met or broke up.

We have heard from a woman who graduated from the Seminary. It is not unfitting to let one of his boys speak. In this case it is Sam

Higginbottom, one of the most useful graduates of Mount Hermon, for his work at Allahabad in founding the Agricultural Institute and the Allahabad Christian College ranks with the contributions made in any field of missionary endeavor of recent years. Only within a few days this old friend, for we were in school together, quite unsolicited and with no knowledge of any activity on my part sent me some recollections. A few of these being new to me, I record.

I left school in Manchester, England, and went to work before my twelfth birthday. The family moved to Wales when I was sixteen. I was converted at seventeen and left Wales for America August 1894, when I was nineteen. I went direct to Mount Hermon School. For the following five years I was in the School and there prepared for college. I also worked in Northfield for three summer vacations on the farm, as porter in the hotel, as clerk, and so on. During my last summer at Northfield, 1899, for the big August Conference, my duty was to sweep the auditorium and keep it tidy. I was to be near at hand during the meetings and run errands and messages for Mr. Moody.

As I think back over the years I would describe Mr. Moody as the most consecrated man I have ever known. He was not ascetic, not "pious"; he impressed one with his tremendous vital energy. He was always utterly unconscious of himself, he never posed; he was beautifully simple and natural. He was truly humble in the best sense, not due to any inferiority complex: very teachable. He loved jokes. He would ask, "Which would you rather, be a bigger fool than you look or look a bigger fool than you are?" To your answer he fairly shook as he answered, "Impossible."

Religiously he was the most tolerant man I have ever met. On the platform at Northfield were gathered High Church, Low Church, Free Church, men of the most diverse theological opinions and heritages; but any man who was honored of God and who was loyal to Jesus Christ as Lord and Saviour was a brother beloved to D. L. Moody. After Mr. Moody's death there were those of his friends who before making some particularly intolerant statement or doing some ungenerous thing would say: "Well, we do this because we are sure Mr. Moody would do it this way." Little they knew Mr. Moody! Never was he intolerant or ungenerous. He often would do the unusual and the unexpected, but it would be tolerant, generous, broad, and big.

The technique of his public speech was as nearly perfect as anything human can be. He knew why Jesus could be heard. He copied Jesus in the Sermon on the Mount, who "opened his mouth" and taught his disciples. This was the first thing noticeable about Mr. Moody when he spoke in public. He opened his mouth. In any large audience he looked for a sympathetic face in the back row and would speak to that one individual, knowing that if that man could hear him then everybody else in the audience who was normal could hear. He never turned to the right or to the left when he spoke. When he read the Bible in public he never left it on the desk and read into the desk, but he picked it up, held it in his hands, high enough up, head high, so that his words would carry over to his audience. He did not have the annoying habit of dropping his voice at the end of his sentences in order to become "impressive." He spoke slowly, deliberately, and was careful of his enunciations. His gestures were very few. In all the things that matter in public speaking he was the most finished artist; yet no one thought of his artistry. His message so consumed him that he too could describe himself as a "Voice." It was so perfectly and unconsciously done.

I remember Mr. Moody's telling us of two poor boys that he put through Mount Hermon. They were good students. He sent them to Yale University, paid all their term bills, and gave them vacation expenses. After they were graduated they wrote and asked him what he was going to do for them then. He wrote back to say that he had done his share and that it was now time they did something for themselves. They wrote to him blistering, scorching letters, such letters as he had never received from anyone, no word of gratitude or thanks. With tears streaming down his face he confessed that he deserved all they said. His was the fault. He had given them a false view of life. He had given them something for nothing. He had fostered the idea that the world owed them something, that they had a right to a living without earning it. He had done them great injury and deserved to suffer.

Mr. Moody was forgiving more than most men. I have been present in the Northfield church when it was crowded. Mr. Moody was the preacher. As he sat on the platform he saw a man in the audience with whom he had quarreled. Leaving Professor Phillips to carry on congregational singing, one hymn after another, Mr. Moody came down from the pulpit, walked down the aisle, called this man out of the pew, and the two walked out of the church. Mr. Moody returned with the man in about fifteen minutes, both of them with changed faces, now happy, smiling, and friendly. Mr. Moody had gone out and settled the quarrel with this man. If his brother had aught against him he had left his gift on the altar and was reconciled to his brother; he settled his difference before he came to the altar to offer his gift.

Mr. Moody brought George Adam Smith over to Mount Hermon once. There never was a more princely host. If there was no other place in the schedule where such a man could speak, Mr. Moody would bring him into the school dining room and have the man speak there. George Adam Smith was brought in at the close of supper. We turned our chairs round and heard a speech, going into details to tell us that Glasgow was undoubtedly the best-governed city in the world. Before he finished we boys had heard so much of the excellencies of Glasgow that we were just sick of it, anxious for him to stop, but he continued to lay it on so thick we could hardly stand it. When he saw that we were restless he turned round and, pointing to Mr. Moody, said, "He is the cause of the civic righteousness of Glasgow, the improvements for the poor and the character of the city, all is due, as far as anything human can be due to any one man, to Mr. Moody." The most perfect tribute I ever saw.

One time my eyes were giving me trouble. I was forbidden to read. Mr. Moody was going out on one of his evangelistic tours. He wanted somebody to go with him to manage a bookstall in his meetings. I went. He was then pushing the Colportage Association. He wanted to get these splendid books, which were sold just at cost price, into the hands of the people. His first meetings were in and about Albany, New York. We got out of the train about seven o'clock on a rainy, sleety morning, dirty and slushy underfoot. There was an old Irishman with white uniform, in his mouth a dirty old clay pipe, sweeping the street at the crossing. As we passed this old street sweeper Mr. Moody gripped him by the hand and said, "Brother, God bless you. We are both engaged in the same work. We are both trying to make this world clean," and passed on. I paused just a moment to tell the old man who it was that had shaken hands with him. His face lighted up with joy and in a rich brogue he said, "Just think of his shaking hands with the likes of me."

Mr. Moody preached very little against superficial things like smoking, card playing, theatregoing, racegoing, drinking, gambling. He did none of them himself and was against them. He was more concerned to preach against the sins of the heart that sour and spoil life — self-righteousness, an unforgiving spirit, pride, back-biting, jealousy, bad temper, unbelief, fear, and laziness. His comment on Spurgeon's remark that "he smoked to the Glory of God" was that smoking to Spurgeon was like a whip to a tired horse. Mr. Moody did not allow smoking or dancing at the Schools. He did not argue about smoking. He said it was an expensive habit. Mount Hermon was for poor boys. A boy who could afford to smoke could go to some other school.

Every boy at Mount Hermon felt that Mr. Moody was personally interested in his fortune and success. The thought of this often governed our conduct. A boy would refrain from doing some unworthy act with the remark, "D. L. Moody would not like it." The same boy would do some beautiful, sacrificial deed and smile and say, "That would please D. L." Mr. Moody had defined character for us, saying, "Character is what a man is in the dark."

Much of my work in India has been colored by the thought, "Well, D. L. would do this sort of thing. He is more interested in me to-day than when we were both at Northfield."

XI

LAST THINGS

At Christmas in 1898 my father and mother were in Colorado and sent for me to come on and spend Christmas with them. Because I had unconsciously expressed a preference for Colorado Springs they arranged to be there, but I was to meet them at Denver. It was shortly after the disappearance of Schlatter, a curious healer who had wrought many cures. Father was keenly interested in interrogating the newspapermen who had covered the incident of the very mysterious and remarkable man, and he was deeply impressed by all he was told concerning him. At that time there came to call, also, a son of a friend of Chicago days. This friend had been through a remarkable experience. My father renewed his impressions of the story, and it was so remarkable that after the caller had left I asked him why he had never told it. His reply was typical. "Would you believe it if you had heard it?" When I hesitated he replied that that was the answer. It would strain his hearers' credulity too much.

Another experience of that visit lingers. He took me to one of his large meetings and told me he was going to call upon me to talk for five minutes and to try to say in those five minutes what I thought it meant to be a Christian. First he called upon two ministers, who each exceeded their time. I was a sophomore at college and the experience was a trying one and I was frightened, but when he called on me I did my humble and sophomoric best. He was good enough to say afterwards that I said more in my five minutes than the others had said in a much longer time. Afterwards I was glad I had complied with his request, for it was the last Christmas he was alive. I came back to New Haven and he and my mother made their way West, sending for my brother and his wife and daughter to join them.

That spring, he was, as I have said, again in

New Haven, on which occasion he met George Adam Smith and invited him to North-field, much to the annoyance of some of his friends, who bothered more about orthodoxy than he did. To make matters worse from their standpoint he asked at the same time S. Parkes Cadman, whose fame was growing and who was entering upon that signally useful ministry which ended only a year ago. A great deal of comment was made on this move of my father's, but it influenced him not one whit. That summer of 1899 was saddened by the death of my brother's oldest daughter, — his first grandchild, — who died at the age of four. We learned afterwards that all summer his heart had given repeated warnings, but he said nothing lest his family worry, and kept on his usual round with unabated energy. In the latter part of the summer, unwilling to ask my brother to carry through some plans which had been made for him, he sent me out on a peculiar mission for a lad of twenty. I was sent to Toronto, Rochester, and Utica to arrange a series of meetings for Campbell Morgan. In each place I had to deal with committees of ministers who, I felt, concealed not too successfully their surprise and displeasure at having to comply with instructions which I was under orders to give. It was a trying time for both the ministers and myself. It was the first administrative responsibility wished upon me and he seemed to feel satisfied by the way I discharged it. At any rate I had the feeling that I was admitted further into his confidence and that he felt I was maturing.

This probably accounts for the fact that that autumn he took me more completely into his confidence than he ever had before. Shortly before he left for Kansas City I came home for the week-end and he invited me to drive to Mount Hermon with him, where he was preaching to the boys. On the drive he referred to the fact that I was now more than halfway through college and inquired my ideas as to my future. I replied that I was leaning strongly toward the ministry. He frowned upon the idea for me. My field of effort, he was persuaded, was not in the ordained ministry or in a regular pulpit or parish, but rather as a free lance like himself. When I pointed out that I did not feel called or fitted in the least for the sort of work he had done, he answered that this was not his idea. He wanted me to be a teacher or expositor of the Bible. I knew that he felt strongly about two Yale men to whom he was attached and had wanted them to avoid the regular routine of pastoral work and give themselves to Biblical exposition. And then quite suddenly and unexpectedly he discussed the immediate future of the work at North-field after he was dead, and discussed as he never had before the qualifications and lack of qualifications of those who were associated with him and hurriedly sketched some of the problems which rested most heavily upon him. If on the one hand I was touched at his apparent confidence in me I was deeply concerned at the manner in which his problems seemed to weigh upon him. A few minutes later this was forgotten as he preached with his usual vigor to the boys of the school. As far as I recall we did not return to the discussion on our way home. But he was in a distinctly thoughtful mood. I think it was the last time he ever spoke at Northfield or Mount Hermon.

The next morning, contrary to his usual custom, he did not drive me to the early train

I had to take, but allowed the man of all work about the house to do this. It was so unusual that I commented upon it mentally, but did not realize that it was a concession on his part to exhaustion, the sense of which was a mounting burden. That week he left for Kansas City, and his collapse there followed after several services. He tried to make light of it but could not. My first intimation of it was the morning paper, which carried headlines of an alarming nature. Telegrams came in from my mother and I met her and my brother at Springfield, where at first it was planned that I should go with them to meet him. Fortunately the plan was altered and I was sent home and they went West, where by mischance they missed his train. Finding that his special car was arriving at Greenfield, a junction twelve miles below our home, I drove down to meet it. We had two pairs of horses — one, as I have said, steady, the other full of life. I chose the steadier pair, under the circumstances, as safer and less apt to become excited, and felt greatly reassured when in his old manner he chided me for having brought the slower horses, which could not cover the distance within half an hour of the other team, and laughed at my old fogeyness in being cautious. He could not endure slow horses. That night on reaching home, after resting a few minutes, he walked up to his room. It was thought wisest that someone should sit up with him and in the absence of my mother and brother this fell to me. And having become used to my presence it was his wish that I should be in his room the second night. After this, as no immediate danger seemed imminent and it was hopefully believed that quiet and rest would restore him, I returned to college. He was still making progress apparently satisfactorily when I returned a week or so later, and we were still hopeful when I returned for the Christmas vacation. He had changed his room and spent a good part of the day in his dressing gown, sitting in a chair and taking a keen interest in the papers, particularly news of the Boer War. He and my brother were pro-Boer and I was not, and we had endless arguments. The night before he died it was determined that I should go down to New York to see the specialist who had come to see him and arrange for a new nurse, the one he had being an efficient but doleful creature he could not abide. By a mistake which was providential I was not aroused in time, so missed the early train, otherwise I should have been away when he died. The day before, I had been alone with him when he had had an alarming fainting spell, and it was very typical of him that the rest of the day he seemed more concerned with my concern, about which he rallied me, than he did about himself, and joked about the unwisdom *for my sake* of leaving me alone in the room with him.

Early that morning the doctor felt he would not last the day out. He was restless in bed and more comfortable in one particular chair, but he was fully aware of everything, especially our alarm, and submitted for a time to the heart stimulants, but finally he brushed these aside, declaring that they were merely prolonging the end and making it harder for my mother, who as always was uppermost in his thoughts. He declared a little while before the end that he had always been ambitious for work and that was all he was leaving us — the work in Chicago to my sister's husband, the work at

Mount Hermon to my brother, and the work at Northfield to me. When he knew he was dying he declared it a glorious experience — not the least to be dreaded. "Earth is receding and Heaven is calling," he almost shouted, and declared he saw his dear grandchildren's faces welcoming him. So he went out, as he had always lived, on flood tide, and we buried him in a spot he had loved both for its views and for its associations, Round Top, from which can be seen the humble farmhouse where he was born and the equally simple house which had been a refuge for a quarter of a century. And there on the stone my brother had inscribed the words, "He that doeth the will of God abideth forever."

XII

IN RETROSPECT

When the eyes have done their part
Then thought must length it in the heart.

FOR nearly forty years two things have been very irritating. One is to see men who to my mind had nothing in common with my father save his enthusiasm called "the Chinese Moody" or "the Patagonian Moody," and so on. The other is dogmatic statements of what he would approve or disapprove to-day, if he were among us. The old game of "if — what?" has never lacked for players. "If Hannibal had had tanks, he would have won the Punic War." "If Napoleon had had machine guns," or "Nelson . . . submarines," or "Lee . . . airplanes," and so forth. It is as futile as it is facile.[1]

[1] This silly "if" business reaches an awful *reductio ad absurdum* in a wretched conundrum of the eighties. "If Rider Haggard had been Lew Wallace, who would *She* have been?" And the incredibly inane answer was, "*Ben-Hur.*" If this is not answering a fool according to his folly!

Dr. Robert E. Speer summed up all this sort of speculation in an address at the closing of the Northfield celebration of the Centenary: —

"If Mr. Moody were back in our world now would he fill the same place in it which he filled between forty and seventy years ago? Would he wield the influence now that he wielded then? Would the multitudes come to hear him to-day as they thronged to hear him in those days, and would he mould and sway the popular mind now as he moulded and swayed it when he walked here more than half a century ago? Would he use the same methods to-day he used then, and if he did would they be futile or would they be effective? Would his message be different now from what it was when he spoke to multitudes across the English-speaking world, or would he alter or abandon some of the convictions which he spoke with such clarity and devotion a generation and more ago? The answer to these questions is both no and yes."

Nevertheless, despite the fact that the answer is yes *and* no, questions of this sort will be asked and perhaps it is natural that they should, and they will be answered in accordance with prejudices and preconceptions of those who raise them. Yet for the benefit of those who ask what my father would do if he were alive to-day, there are several observations which it may be appropriate to make, and which I believe are basic.

It is not to be forgotten that he was a Victorian. He was born a few months before Victoria was awakened early in that dramatic scene. He died a few months before that great reign came at long last to an end. He could not have touched his day as he did had he not been in some respects a son of that day, sharing its prejudices and its viewpoints, respecting many of its taboos and its conventions. But more and more he distinguished between prejudices and principles and his growth in tolerance and forbearance was constant and great.

If human nature has not changed, the physical world in which man lives has changed. I do not know that my father ever saw an automobile, that factor which has so completely

A CHARACTERISTIC POSE

altered so many methods of life, particularly in the city. The airplane has reduced distances and he never saw one. The moving-picture industry, which has grown to such great dimensions, with such bewildering effect on people's tastes and outlook, was hardly in its experimental stage, and he never heard the word "movie" or saw what it has brought in its train. The radio, too, with its tremendous service, was another thing of which he never faintly dreamed. But it is easy to imagine how it would have captured his imagination and enthusiasm as a vehicle for the preaching of the Gospel. It is a different world in many respects into which his grandchildren and great-grandchildren have been born.

Equally great changes have taken place in the world of thought and knowledge. The full import of Darwin and the theory of evolution was not felt until long after the publication of *The Origin of Species* in 1859. Yet my father was actively engaged in mission work by the time it appeared. The full effect of the now forgotten *Essays and Reviews*, which was published in March 1860, was not felt until long afterwards, nor was the work of Bishop Colenso, which in 1862 so cracked the lethargy of the Church of England. There was a wide area in England still unaffected by these things during his first mission in 1873–1875. The famous heresy trial of Robertson Smith (in 1876) actually occurred after his first mission, and with the outcome of this there came a change over the whole Church in Great Britain, a change which may in part account for the fact that the subsequent missions of 1881–1883 and 1891–1892 did not make the same kind of impress, a fact of which my father, despite its denial by others, was I believe fully aware. It is these things, even more than the physical inventions and changes, which separate us from the generation to which he preached.

And to this must be added the great increase in formal education. The word "formal" is used deliberately, for it is not to be taken for granted that our intelligence is necessarily higher because we have remained longer in school or because more have gone to college.

But this has unquestionably made for an increased unwillingness on the part of mankind to take the Bible with the same docility as an ultimate and final authority on as many subjects in life and conduct as did our forefathers. It is by no means as easy now to end an argument or silence an opponent by quoting or even misquoting Scripture as it was once. And there is, despite the fact that more knowledge is available about the Bible, greater ignorance concerning its actual contents. To-day, even though he might preach through the radio to large unseen audiences or actually move larger gatherings through amplifiers, he would find far fewer who understood the Bible he quoted or felt to the extent he did its compelling and arresting authority.

There has also grown in the past generation, at least in certain quarters, a new conscience on many social matters, and our day condemns many things taken for granted in his. It is true that he had little concern with the Social Gospel, so called, declaring often that the heart of the individual had to be changed before a change in his environment took place, and one of his favorite aphorisms was that you could not improve the water supply by painting the pump. But he would have favored painting the pump after the well was cleaned and he would have chosen a bright color. It is true that in his day he was deeply concerned about many matters to which the Church was indifferent.

All these things must be kept in mind in saying what he would or would not do to-day.

But there are certain things that must be said, not about his day or ours, but about the man himself, which should give anyone pause in attempting to label him to-day as liberal or conservative, or daring to say he was a modernist or fundamentalist, or draping his broad shoulders with strange unfitting garments dyed in their own prejudices or preconceptions. In his own day he was usually unpredictable. I think he would be still. I admit I approach this diffidently lest I seem to be attempting an *apologia pro vita sua*, for I have been accused of being a modernist or liberal unfairly, I think. I have even been accused of being untrue to his teachings and beliefs and a traitor to all he held dear. And I think quite untruly and unfairly. But I have tried to emulate his honesty.

Among the considerations for those who would try to say what he would do to-day, I should put first his open-mindedness. Sir George Adam Smith records some of the conversations he had with my father the summer before he died. He and Sir George tried to see each other's viewpoint and while they could not see eye to eye they remained fast friends and strong in their mutual affection and respect. Father repeated again and again that the authorship was a relatively unimportant matter when shown the difficulty of some of the traditional positions, and that what really mattered was the contents. It has always seemed to me a curious anomaly that the very stoutest defenders of the traditional authorship have at the same time been the most ardent advocates of the theory of verbal inspiration. If

183

God dictated every word and every comma, the importance of the actual amanuensis was very small indeed.

Even as a small boy I was impressed by his willingness to listen to what even I had to say or ask, unimportant as it was. As I grew older and took questions to him he was never dogmatic in his answers. I once asked him where he thought the direct discourse ended in the third chapter of John. To my surprise he answered that he *thought* it ended at the fourteenth verse. Then he added that he had formerly thought and would like to think that it was Jesus and not John who uttered the contents of the famous sixteenth verse, so dear to him, "God so loved the world."

His friendship and admiration for Dr. Henry Weston of Crozier Theological Seminary belong to the last chapter of his life. This rare old scholar had never heard my father and had been a little prejudiced against him. But shortly before my father's death he was persuaded to come to Northfield. Father invited him to speak and he replied he was no preacher, only an expositor. So Father immediately asked him to give a series of expositions. This he reluctantly consented to do. It was Father's frequent custom, after introducing a speaker, to carry a chair down off the platform and sit at the speaker's feet. The first time Dr. Weston spoke Father did this, and, unconventional as usual, remarked early in the talk, "There goes one of my sermons." Just a little at a loss over the interruption, Dr. Weston looked down and asked what he meant. My father replied that he had always used that text as though it meant this or that, and Dr. Weston's exposition had shown him he was wrong and he could not use that sermon again. A few minutes later he exclaimed, "There goes another." Dr. Weston's delight knew no bounds. For years he had found fault with the erroneous exegeses of his students in the theological seminary and they had defended their mistakes by quoting sermons of my father's. "Now," said Dr. Weston, "I can answer them," and the two became the best of friends. The incident is, I believe, very typical. I have heard learned men deliberately do violence to a text. If my father ever did this it was in ignorance, and such was his honesty that once aware of it he could never do it again. The truth to him was clear enough in the Scripture without the need of reading in what was not there or doing violence to what was. Surely this was open-minded.

It was because he was open-minded that he continued to grow. Not for a moment can the veracity be questioned of those who tell us of the stories which led to his being called "Crazy Moody" when a young man in Chicago. But by the time I remember him he often publicly deprecated the very things he had formerly done. I remember distinctly his being driven home one afternoon from a junction ten miles away where he had been stranded and where with characteristic impatience he refused to wait. He had hired a livery rig, driven by one of the type usually to be found in those days in livery stables, a type not exactly noted as pre-eminent for piety. He referred to it later in an address to the students. There had been a day, he said, when he would have asked this youth if he was a Christian. Now he knew it was no use attempting questions of this sort until confidence and affection had been won. It has been said he never let a day go by without speaking to someone of his eternal destiny. I do not question this in his early days, but I do know there were countless days in Northfield when we could account for every moment from dawn till dark in which he never had an opportunity, nor made, as far as we could see, any attempt to find one. And I do know that whenever I brought home from college any classmate who was not a Christian, I never needed to be alarmed about awkward questions, or fear lest my friend would be embarrassed. And one and all they were enthusiastic about him, so perfectly did he play the host and further any plans we had.

By all accounts he was not the same man in 1873 that he was in 1883 or in 1893. Even less was he the same man he was in early Chicago days. By the latter date my memories are distinct, and Drummond commented on a change and growth he always felt whenever they met after an absence. "Moody is the same," he would say, "but broader and bigger."

Nor, in asserting what he would do to-day, should his humility be forgotten. The views he held and preached were those he had studied

and heard from men who in his formative days he had admired. Within reach as I write are the commentaries of C.H.M. (C. H. MacIntosh), and Father thought highly of all his work. MacIntosh was one of the leading Plymouth Brethren and to the leaders and teachings of this group Father owed much. But very soon he became too liberal for them and, while never a member, he had less and less to do with them. Their separatist doctrines he could not follow. The Cross of Christ was always centripetal to him in its influence, never centrifugal, drawing men together and not separating them. He was keenly aware of his lack of formal training and he would not pose as a Theologian. He was an Evangelist. Of all the things I have heard since he died I believe he would have rejoiced most in a sentence attributed to Dean Inge. "The Gospel is not good advice. It is good news." The matured findings of devout scholars he would not have brushed aside as some have done, feeling as he did that learning had its place and there was room for the scholar as well as the evangelist in the economy of God. The word of God was to him a two-edged sword. It needed to be used, not to be defended. He never feared for the Ark of the Lord and his faith rested on too solid a foundation to be disturbed by the spade of the excavator as the translation of forgotten lan-

guages on monuments. He had used his faith
and it had worked. Like Saint Paul, whom he
so greatly admired, he could say, "I know
whom I have believed."

Again the growing emphasis on Education
to which he gave more and more of his time
to the end is evidence, if any is needed, that
necessary as he considered conversion, it was
not enough. As the newborn babe needs care
and nurture, so the newborn soul needs training. From his own experience he might be
pardoned if he had been an advocate of an untrained ministry, but he was not, though he
was sorely tried at much of the dryness of the
seminaries of his day. When I went to Scotland
to study, some of the Old Guard felt he would
have disapproved and said so, acidly. But my
mother, who of all knew him best, not only
approved but accompanied me.

He died before the term "fundamentalism"
came to have its present connotation. It is true
that he gave adherence to most of the doctrines
which are regarded as fundamentalist, but

never in his case as separatist doctrines. In the years when he was forming his creed, the great rank and file of the Church accepted these as well as most of the leaders. But from some of these doctrines he moved away imperceptibly and perhaps unconsciously in his thought and in his actions. For example, he held the doctrine of verbal inspiration, and I have heard him say that if the Bible had said Jonah swallowed the whale he would have believed it. Yet when I went to him once with a question raised in a class I was endeavoring to teach as to the two divergent accounts of the death of Judas, his only reply was hardly consistent with strict adherence to this doctrine. With his usual prefatory "Huh," part grunt, part snort, but wholly explosive and reserved for nonsense, he said, "What difference does it make what happened to a rascal like Judas?" Wholly satisfactory and perfectly characteristic, but not an answer to a problem which, while no problem to a liberal and no problem to him, yet remains a problem for the literalist. I am very sure he would never have fallen back on the silly explanation that the rope broke, and I am even more sure he would have snorted again at solemn nonsense about the verbal inspiration of the original manuscripts if we could find them. He did use his own judgment, though he would not have called it critical, and on such occasions the theory went out the window with scant ceremony. His unfailing common sense carried him invariably over and above some things to which he gave assent.

He believed in the Second Coming, loved to preach on it, and one of his favorite poems was on this theme. Yet he built his Schools on a sound and enduring basis, and brick and mortar confounded some of the Old Guard, who, like the Thessalonians to whom Paul wrote, encouraged their listeners to be improvident. For this, despite his theory, my father had scant sympathy. It is common sense again.

As a matter of fact, inconsistencies never worried him greatly, at least in the realm of thought. In the realm of conduct it was another thing and I never knew a man who strove harder or I believe more successfully to be consistent.[1]

Faith was something to live by, not something to argue and become angry about or define. I do not know how many times I

have heard him say, "I want a faith 's got legs 'n c'n run round." But about inconsistencies in creed he refused to worry. He would only

[1] Dr. Elmer Powell of Chester, Pennsylvania, the man who is perhaps the best-informed student of my father, who has made a lifelong and painstaking study of the smallest details, and who has done much patient research in dust-covered reference books, is never tired of saying, "He was a mountain of rectitude." Incidentally, Dr. Powell has done more to clear up inaccuracies in published accounts of my father's life than anyone else. I cannot adequately express my own debt to him.

smile when one was pointed out. They mattered as little as anachronisms. I did not myself hear it, but one of his admirers told me of his putting a watch in Daniel's pocket and no one in the audience seemed to notice or care. He would have laughed when told of it, and determined not to do it again. But he would have forgotten. After his death a lady in a Sunday School class was highly indignant with me for pointing out that the narrative did not say Elijah was carried to Heaven in a chariot of fire. She silenced and demolished me by saying, "I don't care what it says; I heard your father describe the way he leaned over the chariot and waved to Elisha." Literalist? Not much!

If inconsistency in theology did not worry him much, in conduct it did. I have referred to the Old Guard, men who for the most part had a Plymouth Brethren background and who were forever nagging at my father for some of his dangerous friends like Lyman Abbott, Washington Gladden, and Drummond. Their orthodoxy was sometimes hard to bear and his occasional indifference to their ability to expound the Word and correctness of opinion was hard for them to bear. As a boy and a young man I did not like their sermons or their manners. They seemed to feel and act sometimes as if their orthodoxy established a moratorium for them in such matters as accuracy, for example. I think my father knew well that some evangelists have a reputation for, let us say, embroidery in their sermons. Against every dishonesty of this sort he set his face, and this made it harder for him to see some of the things they did. Two different men, neither deep in his confidence, tried in evangelistic services after his death to convey the idea that he had appointed them as his successors. He would have laughed at the very thought of appointing anyone. The prize example of delicacy was reserved for another, who found fault always with my father behind his back while professing friendship. On one occasion when this gentleman became acutely aware that there was not the feverish demand for his services which he considered appropriate to his orthodoxy and eloquence, he resorted to measures better known in the business world. He found out how much the committee had given Father for one series of meetings. He also secured an estimate on the number of conversions, something my father objected strongly to having counted. Then, taking the figures at a mission he had conducted, he printed a neat little folder showing on one side Father's results and in comparison his, working it out carefully on a per capita basis to show that while under the ministration of D. L. Moody it cost — I have forgotten the exact figures, but let us say $7.43 to bring a soul from darkness to light; under his ministration it could be done for $4.92, a saving of $2.51 a soul! And with this masterpiece he circularized the trade, sending it to all ministers he knew who might be dreaming of an awakening of spiritual life in their churches. This man was more critical of the men whom my father brought to Northfield than anyone else. I remember him distinctly for his great and uncontrollable temper. We assumed it uncontrollable, for we never knew it otherwise.

As I look back I see quite clearly that as I grew older, and let us hope more discerning, there were some of this Old Guard whom Father not only did not urge me to go to hear but to whom he did not often listen if he could help it. One who was really a very learned man was preaching one evening when Father did not go. He questioned me on my return and when I told him it was a discussion on the difference between belief "on Christ and belief in Christ," Father grunted. "Just like a Concordance," he said. When I told him once that I did not know what one of his friends was talking about he replied that neither did he! And of another address, very sententious and impossible, he said, when to tease him we asked if he was having it published, "No! There are not enough capital *I*'s in the printing press!"

To believe that, with all his fund of common sense, were he here to-day he would lend allegiance to a separatist body on the one hand, or on the other align himself with a too often sterile liberalism, is too great a stretch of the imagination. It has seemed to me that those who knew him least are readiest to predict what he would say and do. Their certainty is in inverse ratio to their intimacy.

Shortly after I came to Middlebury there appeared in a religious paper a query as to whether, if he were alive at that time, he would be more in sympathy with what was often preached in his name than he would with the platform at Northfield. The proposer of the question believed Northfield would still be nearest his heart and best reflect his spirit. I agreed, and wrote privately to the paper. They asked permission to publish the letter, which was granted. Immediately I was a target for much criticism. This appeared in channels I did not usually see, but one loving friend took pains that I did. While I felt that I had been correct and that the abuse was not entirely deserved, I may have been stung more than I should. But that night I had a dream. Father was in Middlebury buying a house, and asked me to come with him and help him select it. It was all very vivid. Knowing his fondness for Northfield, I inquired why he wanted another house. Then in the dream he looked at me with that wealth of affection I had seen so often in his eyes, and said, "Because I want to be near you." This implied, I felt in the dream, that he knew his work was nearing its end and mine was ahead of me. Then he turned and kissed me as he had done when I was a child, though seldom since then. I felt that rough beard on my face in the dream, and woke with a vivid sense of its resemblance to all my boyhood experiences. I have never worried since when I have been accused by those who never even saw him of not understanding him or of being disloyal to his memory.

BIBLIOGRAPHY

BIBLIOGRAPHY

OVER fifty biographies of my father are in existence. Some are very slight, merely sketches written while the mission in Great Britain was going on in 1873–1875, twenty-five years before his death and before the Schools were founded or later developments arose. These are apt to fall into two classes. One emphasizes the power of God and slights the human element, making it all miracle and undervaluing certain qualities in the man. R. W. Dale of Birmingham, approaching him at first critically, could find in him nothing to account for his success. Yet Henry Drummond declared him the greatest "human" he had known. This class is large. Writers in this group overlook and slight all that does not fall in with their thesis, and they are almost without exception inaccurate and misleading. Everything, according to these writers, was due to the infilling of the Holy Spirit, nothing to the human personality. These writers make much, and possibly rightly, of Henry Varley's sentence which influenced my father, "The world has yet to see what God can do with a man completely consecrated." Yet the human personality cannot be entirely ignored. There have been numerous good men more learned, more eloquent, and equally devoted. If this is so why have there not been hundreds of others with a similar story? It is a legitimate question. For the most part these biographies are silly and partial, inaccurate and falsely pious. Some of this trashy, erroneous, and almost invariably sensational rubbish is still being published and, I fear, read. The sane, devoted, radiant soul my father was is misrepresented by those who insist on emphasizing what he minimized and neglecting what was most important to him. They lose him in the attempt to confine him in a doctrinal strait jacket, at which he would have smiled tolerantly in some cases, in others indignantly repudiated.

The other, a much smaller group, have gone

almost equally erroneously to the other extreme and endeavored to account for everything in my father's life on purely human grounds. The task is much too great for them, and the reader puts books of this kind down with the feeling that the story has not been told.

He would have preferred that no biography be written. The rise of unauthorized and unauthentic biographies annoyed him. Shortly before his death an associate asked permission to write one. My father refused and said at that time if a biography had to be written he wanted my brother to do it, and it was clearly understood by the family that this was his wish. On his death a biography was announced as authorized by the very individual to whom permission was refused. No access was had to any papers or letters in the possession of the family and it appeared in the face of protests from the family.

My brother undertook the task twice. The first time he was rushed into it by the advice of those he trusted. On his shoulders had fallen

the responsibility for all the work at Northfield, summer and winter. He was thirty years
old and handicapped in many instances by the
assistance of some who were more in the nature of liabilities than assets. The book appeared the year following my father's death,
much too soon. It was a very much better book
than my brother would ever allow, but he
never rested until thirty years later he had
done it again. By that time he was a sick man.
But he summoned his strength to the task and
completed his work of thirty years. In a sense
he lived for this, reading constantly to this
end. It is the one complete and authoritative
biography of my father, and the one to which
future students of his life must turn for accurate information.

My brother struggled hard to make it as objective as possible. This is a hard task under
any circumstances and an almost impossible
one for a son so devoted as my brother. As
I read the manuscript for him as well as the
proofs I wondered he had done as well as he
had. But it was a great handicap under which

to struggle, his passionate admiration and love for my father. No man ever had a more devoted son, and while by temperament they differed they were alike in their large-heartedness and their fidelity to their convictions.

My brother-in-law, Mr. A. P. Fitt, has essayed it twice, once in 1900 and once in 1936. These are short compact lives — and valuable for their condensation. And they are accurate. They are less attemptedly objective than my brother's. My brother-in-law was as deeply devoted in his way as my brother and was with Father constantly the last seven years of his life.

Two studies have been made of my father which any student of his life must consider. One is by his lifelong friend, Henry Drummond. It was written in response to a request from Mr. S. S. McClure, and I remember well Mr. McClure's visit to Northfield to secure Drummond's consent to the project. It appeared in two articles in *McClure's* in 1893 and 1894. It was written while my father was alive and it is as warm in its appreciation as one my father would have written of Drummond. It is an intimate sketch by one of Father's most prized friends, if not the most prized of them all. It appeared in book form in 1900, prefaced by Sir George Adam Smith, and the preface is one of the most discriminating and beautiful tributes to my father of which I know.

The other study is Gamaliel Bradford's, one of his psychographs. Bradford was a professed agnostic, a wistful one, but nonetheless for this reason dealing with a difficult subject. The remark of the woman at the well in the fourth chapter of John comes back as one reads it, "Sir, thou hast nothing to draw with, and the well is deep." Despite an unconsciously patronizing and often condescending tone which makes certain inaccuracies and, to me, perfectly unsupportable surmises all the more unendurable, the book is valuable. Bradford confesses elsewhere a bewilderment in writing it which he did not feel in his other psychographs. But in this class, the class which denies more than a human basis, this is the best.

BIBLIOGRAPHY

Mention should be made of the biography by Charles Goss, an associate of whom my father was particularly fond. It was published in 1900, too hurriedly, but it contains much valuable information not generally found elsewhere and which can be relied upon, and at the end contains a number of sermons which for accuracy of reproduction seem to me to surpass any of the other published collections. These sermons are less ghost-written and more as they were delivered.

The best purely subjective book I know of — it is hardly a study — is a little book privately printed by Mrs. Peter McKinnon. Mr. and Mrs. McKinnon were active workers in all my father's meetings from the first, warm personal friends and ardent supporters of his work everywhere. They were hosts to my father on his visit to Palestine, and Mrs. McKinnon kept voluminous diaries and notes. These go to make up a series of reminiscences not without great charm and color, with a veritable note of authenticity.

The host of smaller books and magazine

209

articles there is not room to mention. In my judgment the best of the shorter studies are those by John McDowell and Charles R. Erdman. The former saw much of Father both while he was a student and later. Dr. Erdman and his father were closely associated with my father and knew him well. R. L. Duffus wrote a notable article for the *American Mercury* in April 1925, and G. Glenn Atkins has written some excellent articles in various places.